BETWEEN THE SUNSET
AND THE STARS

Also by E. M. Blaiklock

Commentary on the New Testament
Blaiklock's Bible Handbook
Kathleen
Still a Christian

Translations:

The Imitation of Christ
The Practice of the Presence of God

BETWEEN THE SUNSET AND THE STARS

E. M. Blaiklock

HODDER AND STOUGHTON
LONDON SYDNEY AUCKLAND TORONTO

British Library Cataloguing in Publication Data

Blaiklock, E. M.
    Between the sunset and the stars.
1. Old age   2. Adjustment (Psychology)
I. Title
261.8'3426   HQ1061

ISBN 0 340 27602 9

Hodder and Stoughton Editorial Office: 47 Bedford Square, London WC1B 3DP

CONTENTS

Foreword

I once wrote out a verse I found upon a sundial in an old Essex church. Perhaps you know it. It runs:

When, as a child I laughed and wept,
                    Time crept.
When as a youth I dreamed and talked,
                    Time walked.
When I became a full-grown man,
                    Time ran.
And later as I older grew,
                    Time flew.
Soon I shall find while treading on,
                    Time gone.

I quote by way of explanation. In the last few years I have been drawn into autobiography. Kind people have said they were glad. We all like a whiff of the past, a peep at the personal. At the same time we should not survive simply to reminisce, much less to do other than instruct. This, then, is possibly my last book of such content. I am surely of an age to write it and, it seems, I should.

By Way of Introduction

In the more courtly days of literature there was a practice of writing what was called an envoi, to speed a book upon its way. It was sometimes the last stanza of a poem; sometimes, though written last, it became a preface or an introduction. Illustration could range from the first Psalm to Catullus and Saint Luke.

With serious intent or mock apology, the writer sent his book to face its readers. Not without a touch of apprehension, he committed his nursling to the kindly eyes of friends and the less partial scrutiny of others.

I do no less with what I have been bold enough to write on the experience of age. I have reached no conclusions which I might not have reached half a lifetime back, but I now begin to don responsibility. If ever I am to speak it must be now. And that is a point perhaps still open for reproof.

With an hour to spare before bedtime, I took down a charming novel about an old scholar which first held me when I was a boy in Paris in 1924. It is *The Crime of Silvestre Bonnard* by Anatole France. Quite by chance I opened it half way through, here in my own 'Cité de Livres'. I quote: 'One day last year one of my fellow-members at the Institute was lamenting over the boredom of getting old. "Still," Saint-Beuve replied to him, "It is the only way that has yet been found of living a long time." '

My envoi then. Go small book, and may you meet an aching need.

E. M. Blaiklock
Titirangi
Auckland

6 July, 1981

Chapter One

GREEN OLIVE TREES

I can see the old gentleman now. He must have been nearer ninety than eighty years of age. His gnarled brown hands were clasped one over the other on top of a knobbled stick, 'a grievous crabtree cudgel', as I would say to myself, remembering Giant Despair's weapon in the woodcut in our big leather-bound *Pilgrim's Progress* at home – round the corner up the lane, a lovely lane in those days, tunnelled under trees.

There was no despair about old Mr Denyer. His eyes were bright as he sat on the sturdy wooden bench on the front verandah of the grey house under the huge pines. It was the edge of town, where the first orchard planting of the pioneers paused before the southwestern wilderness. He was one of those who set the pears and apples in the clay, circled them with the resin-scented trees, and built himself the timbered cottage.

I would go in as I neared home after the long walk from school, and talk to him of those days when the first settlers came to the valley, when lonely gumdiggers probed and delved for fossil gum, the blood of vanished kauri woods, about the fears they had of a Maori attack up the narrow neck of land between the twin harbours of Auckland. . . . And he might turn to present times and speak with concern about the young men in khaki about town again, as he remembered them fourteen years before, when they were sent off to fight the obstinate Boers, and there were places like Ladysmith and Kimberley in the news, and the streets went mad over the relief of Mafeking.

I sat on the edge of the verandah, and he fascinated me

11

with all he could remember as he looked past his rose bushes and ordered rows of beans and cabbages into other years. I told him tales of school, where the maps hung on the wall with the Empire all in red. We talked about the war which had fallen on us, with Germany attacking 'little Belgium', so tiny on those maps, and the infamous Turks acting as one might expect them to act. Had we not heard of them two years before in the Balkans, and what had Mr Gladstone said about Armenia? It was yesterday to Mr Denyer.

That is how I remember our last conversation. It must have taken place late in our southern spring in 1914, before the first winter congealed the northern battlefields. I called in to talk to him of our latest victory, for even Mons was to us a triumph. The 'Russian steamroller' was lumbering into the hostile East Prussian plains. No Tannenberg yet, and the same doughty allies had smashed a treacherous Turkish attack on the southern Caucasus at a place called Sarikamish.

I cannot find the name on my largest atlas today, or in any reference books I have, but recall drawing my old friend's attention to it, and telling how I had added 'the Battle of Sarikamish' to my list of inevitable successes in the field. 'Yes,' he said, 'for casualties like that I expect the Russians used their guns from the valley-head. They were always good with cannon. I was quite a young man when they were fighting us, and Lord Cardigan charged their batteries down a valley like that, in the Crimea. They shot his Light Brigade to pieces, only six hundred of them.'

I never saw him again. A few days later, on my way home, I stopped in horror at the place. The house was gone, and a square of deep ashes and twisted roofing-iron surrounded a cracked brick chimney. The rose bushes were burned away. The vegetables stood seared and yellow. Some of the tall pines were scorched brown. Where the old man went I never discovered, but he left a sad little gap in my small life.

That was my first contact with old age, and its influence never left me. As an only child of thirteen years, plucked at the age of six from urban Birmingham, and growing up all

12

through the sensitive years of boyhood near Auckland's forested and hilly southwest wilderness, scrub-filled and still scarred by the timber-looting of the pioneers, I saw more of adult society than most of my contemporaries. I sought, but never managed to replace old Mr Denyer, even by another veteran of my acquaintance, a tall Frenchman with a white imperial moustache, who had worn his kepi and carried a chassepot during the Prussian siege of Paris in 1870 and 1871. I had no sense of a generation gap with him either, yet it was the other patriarch who bridged for me the sixty years between Sebastopol and Sarikamish, and who above all preserved me from ever thinking of the aged as a race apart, an alien generation.

Of course, I had young friends in those years of boyhood, but of necessity I spent much time in my own company in solitary exploration of hills and bushland and of the empty beauty of the harbour foreshore over the adjacent ridge beyond the little farm. I am sure that it is true that, before the age of sixteen years, an active mind has encountered in fundamental form all the important questions of life and death which it is likely to meet in its whole span of years. I met foolish old age in those early years, and no long lapse of years can soothe or solace that. I also met idiotic youth and thoughtless middle age, but it never occurred to me to confuse folly with years. This was the measure of my debt to the old gentleman on the verandah, leaning, like Jacob, in the New Testament phrase, 'on the top of his stick'.

So it has been that I do not remember a time in my experience in which I have not been aware of the totality of life, the passing of the years and the strange incompleteness of all earthly things. I have been fortunate. I have swept the gamut of life's best experience and felt the pulse of eternity. I have known, to be sure, the mind's strife, the stress of misfortune, doubt's subtle onslaught, the outworking reality of a wise Plan, the tug and sustenance of all which makes the joy and pain, the peace and poignancy of living. But am I not now about this task because I have always been aware, sometimes dimly, often in urgent clarity, of what the Preacher bids in the tumultuous imagery of the last chapter of Ecclesiastes, 'Remember your Creator in the days of your youth. . . .' I have always known I should one day be old, and have looked, never with scorn, always with compassion and reverence, upon age.

'I am older today,' says the Lady, in Lewis's beautiful and perceptive *Perelandra*, 'yesterday I was younger, and did not understand.' I was once made strongly aware of that swift maturing, and suddenly felt older and a little apart from the other thirty boys who sat with me in the fifth form English class at Auckland Grammar School. It was in 1919, and in that winter term we had the most sensitive of English teachers. He opened for me, amid much else, Tennyson's two poems on old men, Tithonus and Ulysses. Tithonus asked for immortality but forgot to ask for immortal youth. Broken, beaten by the years, he wandered Aurora's halls, 'a white-haired shadow, roaming like a dream'. But there was Ulysses, up and fighting, feet firm-planted, determined not to be cabined by a barren isle, but 'to seek, to find, to strive and not to yield', convinced that there was 'some work of noble note' that age still could accomplish.

It was five years since old Mr Denyer had passed out of my life, and at that time I was traversing a period of uncommon stress, deep disappointment and lonely decision, and those two poems somehow locked with my mood. They have always meant much to me and perhaps that is why the 'strong Hours', living hostile beings who beat Tithonus down, have brought me no surprises.

Indeed they have given me more than I expected of them, and it is only with a mere touch of withered old Tithonus's weariness that the evening shadows lengthen. In my sturdier moods I am more conscious of the brave Ulysses, fretting at the narrowness of Ithaca. That, too, was not quite contrary to my expectations, and a condition for which I early sought to discipline my mind.

I have found astonishingly true some words which my father spoke to me late in his life – that in the evening we are very much what we were in the morning and afternoon of life. If life is a preparation for eternity, it is well, therefore, to remember the edges of eternity and to prepare for them. The Preacher speaks to the point: 'Remember your Creator in the days of your youth, before the days of trouble come, and the years approach when you shall say, "I find no pleasure in them." '

The pessimism of the last words I do not accept, but if Solomon was the Preacher (and there is no valid reason to disbelieve that) I can understand why age was dolorous to him. But it is a fact that God, honoured in youth, can beautify old age, and also supremely true that 'some work of noble note' can still be found to do. I should otherwise see little purpose in thus writing.

Also that explains my conviction that age is not entirely biologically determined. Much of it all is in the mind, and Ulysses' will to live. That is why I chose my sixty-third year to write a monograph on a dialogue on old age from the most eloquent of the Romans, the orator and statesman Cicero, 'Rome's least mortal mind', as Byron called him. He, too, was in his sixty-third year and not far from his death at the hands of the murderous assassins of Mark Antony, against whom, in his finest hour, he had recently vainly fought to save the Republic. It was always a favourite book with me and has often been translated.

Cicero was conscious of no diminution of his mental powers. It was his instinct to resist old age, which, as a Roman of that century, he felt was upon his heels. That is why, he says, in his moving little book, he did not choose Tithonus as his spokesman in the dialogue, an old man longing to be gone, but Cato, whose eighty-four years covered what Cicero thought was the great era of Roman republican glory from near the middle of the third to the middle of the second century before Christ. He died before the beginning of the Time of Troubles which engulfed the writer himself.

And now, rejected by the new forces which assailed the state, excluded from affairs, faced suddenly with old age within, Cicero set out to fight back for his own mind's peace. He made a splendid case for continuing vitality. 'The composition of this book,' he wrote to his friend, 'has been so delightful, that it has not only wiped away all the annoyances of old age, but has even made it an easy and a happy state. Philosophy, therefore, can never be praised as much as she deserves, since she enables a man who is obedient to her precepts to pass every season of life free from worry.' He wrote much in those months of despairing withdrawal which followed Julius Caesar's murder on the Ides of March in 44 BC. It was a great programme of mental effort which has something to offer for a rootless society in another age. Cicero proved that old age can be an Indian summer, given a sound mind. The dotards of the comic stage were never his ideal. An aged fool was a fool in his opinion because he had willed it so by sloth and culpable ineptitude. 'No lapse of time,' he concluded, 'however long, can solace or soothe a foolish old age.'

I suppose it is to be confessed that I wrote the small monograph on Cicero's book because, with my own retirement looming, after a lifetime of fellowship with the great minds of three ancient civilisations, a breath of apprehension had brushed my consciousness. I need not have feared, but as I end fourteen years of another chapter, a new era in my life, I feel grateful to Cicero, and to One Greater than he.

It was a century later that the sardonic satirist, Juvenal, chose to write on senility in his Tenth Satire. 'What,' asked that embittered man, 'is the use of praying for long life?' All Italy thronged the temples when the great Pompey was desperately ill with malaria. He was spared – for what? – to die a refugee at the hand of a brute who had once served under him. And Nestor, Homer's famed old counsellor, who lived to see his son's beard flare upon the pyre. . . . It is possible for one who has lived long with an author to watch his mind at work, and as I pointed out, half a dozen allusions show that Juvenal was thinking about Cicero. Determined to show the other side, he continues: 'How unbroken are the miseries of age. Look at the misshapen and distorted face, so different, the unsightly hide which serves as skin. Young men differ but old men look alike. Their voices are as shaky as their limbs, heads without hair, noses drivelling. . . .' and so on as offensively as untrue. Age can be handsome, keen, with strength unseen in youthful faces.

Surely functions fail, arteries silt, teeth, eyes, ears do reveal the wearing of the years. Vital organs become something less than what they were. But properly conserved and unabused, vigour of body can enter the seventies, perhaps the eighties, almost intact. Live tissue behaves always like tissue, and that is why muscles can still be strengthened by exercise, toned and made to function while they live. True enough, old Tithonus's foes, the 'strong Hours' do 'beat us down and mar and waste us,' as he lamented in Tennyson's poem, but for all the struggle it must be remembered that Shakespeare's parody is not final truth about the

> *lean and slippered pantaloon,*
> *With spectacles on nose, and pouch on side,*
> *His youthful hose, well saved, a world too wide*
> *For his shrunk shank, his big manly voice,*
> *Turning again towards childish treble, pipes*
> *And whistle in its sound; last scene of all,*
> *Which ends this strange eventful history,*
> *Is second childishness and mere oblivion;*
> *Sans teeth, sans eyes, sans taste, sans everything. . . .*

– let us, I beg, remember that modern medicine has first of all alleviated or removed such vast indignities but, more important than that, a battered frame has still the wealth of vivid life within. The very context of Shakespeare's seven ages of man contains old Adam, gentle, valiant, and served well by Orlando: 'How now, Adam! No greater heart in thee. Cheer thyself a little. Thy conceit is nearer death than thy powers. For my sake, be comfortable; hold death awhile at the arm's end. . . . and if I bring thee not something to eat, I'll give thee leave to die, but if thou diest before I come, thou art a mocker of my labour. . . . Cheerily, good Adam.'

The faithful and valiant old man is, in fact, a common character in all drama, back to the Greeks. We so commonly are as we have been, and if a man's brain has been fed, used, kept subtle with exercise, nourished by the life of the soul, it continues so to act as it always acted. In an alien, failing or damaged physical frame the brain can function with all the strength and power of more physically vigorous years. The intellect can remain a synthetising and creative force. If its wondrous mechanism has through all the years been stored and programmed, then apart from massive trauma to its multitudinous cells, it can work on and produce long past the more visible weathering of other bodily systems, and if the living power of the mind is preserved, then the major motive for living, the chief source of continued usefulness, goes on. And if the point of all this is that old age is as much a psychological as a biological phenomenon, the whole process of preservation is within reach of the will, a blessing even if that is denied other parts of the body which can fail and fade beyond all our endeavour.

The brain can be exercised like the muscles. Its survival as a guiding and integrating force can be promoted by determination and an attitude of forward-looking will. And those who have sought to do so will say that never, at any time of life, were they so conscious of that Something Else which makes us living souls, a kind of realised dichotomy of body and mind, of flesh and spirit. 'Rejoice, O young man, in thy youth. . . .' to quote the Preacher again, yes, in the smooth play of limbs, the muscles' running – like Browning's David:

> Oh, the wild joys of living! the leaping
> from rock to rock,
> The strong rending of boughs from the fir-tree,
> the cool silver shock
> Of the plunge in a pool's living water. . . .

We knew it once, but now are fortunate to keep a lance-straight back like my old soldier of the Paris siege, and to look level at the world. . . .

But age has its compensating joys of the wind-swift thought, the thrill to beauty, and even if it is sometimes far from the quietness Rupert Brooke imagined ('that un-hoped serene that men call age'), it has a confidence of understanding, a seeing into the heart of things, a strength called wisdom which brings a satisfaction as profound as any which can come from the functioning of the body in its prime. None can avoid such annoyances as shortening sight, the telephone book becoming more difficult to read without the optometrist's devices and 8 blending exasperatingly with 3, but disciplined habit can go far to remembering those numbers, recalling names with past promptitude, avoidance of repetitive anecdotes, talking too much – all of which small faults of mind can, in fact, be faults of any decade.

Old age is a greater likelihood for the general mass of us than it ever was before. There are in the world at this moment more people who can look forward to many years past the Psalmist's 'three-score years and ten', than at any other time in history. There were then less defences against the tools and powers of death, but those who did attain advanced age in earlier centuries than this made some remarkable contributions to the human story.

Consider John, the apostle of the Lord. He was born at the very beginning of the first century and survived almost until its end, dying about the time when his persecutor Domitian was assassinated, in the middle of the last decade. He must have been around the age of ninety-five when he wrote the Fourth Gospel. Apart from any consideration of its sacred text, that book is a major contribution to ancient literature.

It is brilliant in its story-telling. Witness the Passion and the Resurrection narratives, the scene at Lazarus's tomb, the evocation of atmosphere in the story of John the Baptist by Jordan, the woman at the Sychar well, Nicodemus, who 'came by night', and received so allusive an answer. The irony in the account of the blind man before the Sanhedrin, the power of the scene in the upper room with Judas going out into the night – they are all fine pages of Greek historiography, vivid in their condensed detail. Sense too the power of the mind which could catch up a concept of the writer's fellow Ephesian of six centuries before, that of the Logos or 'the Word', the Vast Intelligence behind phenomena, which expressed itself in the cosmos and in Christ, and compacted Christianity into an eighteen-verse Prologue. John, like Paul, was a man of two cultures. Thus, the last surviving member of Christ's band made his enormous contribution to the faith in his middle nineties.

We may not be able to claim John, the son of Zebedee, as the oldest writer in the ancient world. Sophocles of Athens, who died in 406 BC with 123 plays to his credit, at least comes near to disputing the claim, for some say he lived to be a centenarian. A remarkable story is told of the old tragedian, perhaps the greatest whom that Golden Age of Athens produced. In the last year of his life, when he was at least ninety, Ariston, his eldest son, impatient for his patrimony, brought an action against Sophocles alleging incapability of managing his own affairs. Leaning on the arm of his favourite grandchild, like blind Oedipus in a play he had just written (set in beautiful Colonus, the Athenian suburb of his birth) the old man made no attempt to defend himself against the unfilial charge, but recited a lovely ode from the play which was to be his last. Before he had finished reciting the lines, the jury broke into tumultuous applause. A dotard, they declared, could not have written such words. The charge was thrown out. Listen to just twenty lines of that superb ode which the aged Sophocles read:

Stranger, thou art standing now
On Colonus' rocky brow;
All the haunts of Attic ground,
Where the matchless coursers bound,
Boast not, through their realms of bliss,
Other spot as fair as this.

Mourns the warbling nightingale,
Nestling 'mid the thickest screen
Of the ivy's darksome green.
....

Here Narcissus, day by day,
Buds in clustering beauty gay:
....

Here the golden crocus gleams,
Murmur here unfailing streams,
Sleep the bubbling fountains never,

Feeding pure Cephiseus' river,
Whose prolific waters daily
Bid the pastures blossom gaily,
With the showers of spring-tide blending,
On the lap of earth descending.

The lists of such enduring veterans are long. Thomas à Kempis, the author of the famous devotional book, *The Imitation of Christ*, died at the age of ninety-two, surely the oldest of all his fifteenth-century contemporaries. It would appear that man's basic capacity for length of days has not varied over the centuries. An individual is genetically conditioned to live long or not, and if one could survive the ordeals of plague, pestilence, pollution, starvation, cold and the manifold sources of early decease in disease-ridden cities, famine-ridden years and all the formidable rest of death's occasions, one could be a centenarian then as now.

Fontenelle was. He, Bernard le Bouvier de Fontenelle, nephew of the great dramatist Corneille, French philosopher and poet, and, in the sharp judgment of Voltaire, the most universal genius of his age, lived from 1657 to 1757, and professed to be as happy in his tenth decade as he had ever been. Be that as it may be, such old men do seem to prove again the point that old age is a psychological as well as a biological condition, and that given a certain quota of biological equipment it can be successfully resisted by the brave.

Consider the aged Simeon and Anna, whose story Luke no doubt heard from the aged Mary, when he was collecting material for his gospel, while Paul was in Rome's protective custody in the garrison port of Caesarea. And meet Barzillai whose son, on a shrewd guess, may have been the founder of the shepherds' khan at Bethlehem where Jeremiah found refuge and Christ was born. He was in his middle eighties when he so doughtily served his king.

Or old Caleb, the son of Jephunneh. His brave story is told in the fourteenth chapter of Joshua's story. He was also in his eighties, as strong now as he was in his prime. There was highland country in front of them and he said to Joshua: 'Give me this hill country and I will clear the

Anakim tribesmen from it. I fear them no more now than I did before our desert wanderings when Moses sent me to spy out the land ahead of the host.' And that is what the old man did, and thus it was that the ridge along which the north–south highway runs today, where Hebron stands, became the inheritance of Caleb the Kenezite.

At the end of one of his darker psalms David wrote: 'I am like a green olive tree in the house of God.' In fact David had a sad and premature old age, and the last pages of his story make sombre reading. He had pictured himself, it seems, as enduring and aged when he ended thus Psalm 52. Olives live to immense old age, springing up indomitably from their everlasting roots, whatever despite befalls their trunks and branches. The olive is the living symbol of indestructible vitality. It flourishes in the most inhospitable environment. It never gives in. Its most fruitful years are between the ages of eighty and one hundred and twenty years. Communities in the ancient world depended on the olive. The middle and eastern Mediterranean could not do without it today. Here then is the badge for age. The world needs its olive trees.

Chapter Two

LEICESTER SQUARE AND LUDGATE HILL

We begin to age physically, they say who know such facts, from somewhere in the middle twenties. I am no anatomist and have nothing to say of that. But every one of us can see that some wear out, quite apart from the damage of life, more rapidly than others. Hereditary factors play a part, even in those who have not been foolishly prodigal with their body's health, and those who know must again be left to provide an explanation. That has already been admitted.

But quite apart from failing limbs and cluttered arteries, and that bodily wear which, mercifully, is sometimes not beyond the physician's aid, there is obviously a parallel process in which the mind and heart can wither. David, son of Jesse, closed the last chapter, and David lived too long, although he can hardly have been past his seventy years, lived indeed to survive his honour, the tranquillity of his home, the glory of his psalms, lived to be a senile pawn in clever Bathsheba's hands, as perhaps he had been from the hour when she contrived that he should see her from the palace roof and mar the afternoon of life.

David came to power after years of agonising toil. Suddenly there were no more demands on life and energy. He retired, if that is the word, too soon. The court surrounded and smothered him. It is possible to see the Eastern despot emerging. He was content to leave the leadership of his troops to the sinister Joab, and it was while he loitered in his palace that Bathsheba snared him. Briefly galvanised to life when Absalom rebelled, he wrote some of his most moving psalms, but that whole story reveals a man more tolerated than revered. And Absalom himself was the product of a liaison which never should have been. There was a moral malady in the great guerrilla leader, in the great poet's life. What part that unsurrendered corner played in ageing him can only be our guess.

Life challenges the mind as well as the muscles. Man must resist gravity to live. The body's fibres strengthen by exercise. To float weightless would be to deny health and vigour to the physical frame. And to avoid all confrontation to the soul, the spiritual part of us, and to the thinking mind, is a path to another sort of death.

I saw a sight, infinitely sad, in London last year. It was a hot day in late summer and I had strolled west to say 'goodbye Leicester Square'. I have done that more than once, but always seem to come back to the old grey town again. It was lunchtime, and Londoners of a dozen nations had sought rest for an hour under the heavy green shade of the venerable trees. I was alone, a little sad, and I watched with interest and compassion the hundreds passing by or sitting there, small islands, all of them, of their own joys and sorrows. They would come again tomorrow – and I should be near Bombay – and the next day. I thought of T. S. Eliot watching the fog-smeared host streaming over London Bridge and remembering the lines of Dante: 'I would not have believed that death could have undone so many.' So easily does poetry form a frame for thought.

Whereat, breaking in upon my musing, Death appeared. A tall and haggard boy came in from the direction of Charing Cross Road. He weaved down the diagonal path, stumbling a little, and made towards me, paused glassy-eyed, swaying on his feet and said: 'This is not what that was.' His face had something left in it which suggested twenty-five years, but something else overlaid it which suggested sixty-five. 'This is not what that was,' he mumbled again. 'No, dear boy,' I said, 'but it can be. There is a way back. You can even be born again.' 'No, no,' he said, and staggered out of my life. 'This is not what that was.' Not like glad childhood, no, not what life had offered, no. It was age, horribly precipitated. Life was used up, ending.

Drugs, you will say, and there were a dozen like him up in Piccadilly Circus. His brain was poisoned. It was physical damage. True. But how can we tear apart mind and brain, the structures through which that which is intangible mingles with the tangible it uses? That poor boy had somehow used up life and, like Dorian Gray in Oscar Wilde's grim story, was showing in form and features the death that had been extending grip and tentacle through the essential self long since. The point? Simply this – ageing, I repeat, is a process of the spirit and can be promoted, furthered by a person's own actions, flaccid will, and refusal to confront the toughening challenges of life.

The old marquess in Galsworthy's *Forsyte Saga* put it well to his loose-living granddaughter, Marjorie Farrar: 'I'm eighty, and you're – what are you – twenty-five? Don't get through life so fast – you'll be dreadfully bored by the time you're fifty, and there's no greater bore than a bored person.' I remember the doyen of English poets speaking along the same lines in 1969 at a literary convention in Weston-super-Mare. 'If they're bored now,' said Auden of a younger generation, 'they'll be in hell in ten years' time.'

But to return to the old aristocrat, deciding to sell his precious Gainsborough to pay Marjorie Farrar's debts. He might have said much more. It is not boredom which the rest of us fear in the burnt-out speedsters of a rootless stratum of society. It is the menace they carry for our very survival. The marquess had nothing to offer his worthless granddaughter but a code of decency, surviving, as codes do briefly, from the stabler society and the faith which gave them birth. When the residual ethics die, as they must, what is there to restrain hands which snatch prematurely at remaining life, and snatching find them close on nothing.

Galsworthy, of course, had nothing more himself to say. He was of Shropshire's own generation, and his Forsyte series of novels covered the whole generation through which the Kaiser's war drove its arid swathe of scorched earth. It is here that he fell short. Dechristianised as those times were, and malodorous with a rot of disillusionment, there were Christian forces surviving, but not a Christian intrudes in the Saga. It is a grave lack.

'Don't get through life so fast'. . . . The point is that life can be sapped of savour before it produces fruit. It can be poisoned by venoms of its own generating which it can carry to the grave. That is an odd verse in Job: 'His bones are full of the sin of his youth, which shall lie down with him in the dust.' I know well enough that the King James Version rendering of Job 20:11 leaves something to be desired, and that half a dozen modern translations make the verse much less awesome to read. There are one or two places in that monument of English where a less than accurate translation has left a memorable phrase in the language – for example: 'The iron entered into his soul', as the happy mistranslation of Psalm 105:18 puts it – and the Job passage is one of them. A life envenomed with evil can carry on that evil unpurged, until it ages the body and perverts the mind, mars the very face, and corrupts thought and speech – and accompanies its host to the grave. If, in fact, the ageing process begins in the tissues of the body in the middle twenties, the same movement starts its operation in the fabric of mind and spirit at the same time or sooner. A solemn truth is that.

Byron, who died at the age of thirty-six, had already written:

> *My days are as the withered leaf,*
> *The flower and fruit of life are gone,*
> *The worm the canker and the grief*
> *Are mine alone.*

He died of some fever born of the swamps of Missolonghi, but he was already dead in spirit of a deeper malady. He had lived life 'too fast', and if compassion looks on the generation of the later books of the Forsyte Saga, it senses the desperation of those who saw the slaughter of the war, of the millions deprived of the years yet to be, and who like the Jews of Jerusalem as Sennacherib rolled murderously down upon them said: 'Eat drink and be merry for to-

26

morrow we die'. There is similar despair abroad today, and youth so darkened can only evoke yearning pity.

It is none the less folly so to spill the years. Fruit, in orchard and in life, can be spoiled and tasteless because of unripe plucking. How true is that of the delicacies of love, how true of all living. There must be a reserve, something to work for, an anticipation placed in a hoped tomorrow. Middle age is meant, in divine Providence, to be a projection of youth. Vigour is undiminished. Are not the best marathon runners men entering middle age? Middle age is the time when life's fruits begin to ripen, and the fruit can spoil like the apple I picked the other day from a lichen-hung neglected tree in a corner I no longer tend. A codling moth had planted an egg in the blossom during spring, and black ruin lay at the heart of the fruit. Youth's folly can likewise turn the sturdy years to black dust. Of what value is a flower which cannot turn to seed or fruit? Of what use is mere knowledge if it does not change to wisdom? Or pleasure which spawns pain?

As middle age must be envisaged and prepared for so, too, returning to our theme, must man prepare for old age. In the totality of days we must beware what we store in the personality. It is 'out of the fulness of the heart that the mouth speaks', and more than that – it is out of the same source that thinking comes and inevitably action, for all we do has origin within. Put it in other words. We think, speak and act in accordance with that which, for good and ill, has been stored away in the core of the personality. The deeds we do, the words we say, the thoughts we secretly think, the books we read, the memories we create, all find deposit there. A man once told me how he callously laughed once at a deed of shame and cruelty. 'Hardly a day goes by,' he sighed, 'but that laugh comes back like a lash across my face.'

I can draw no rules for conduct here. I only know, indeed we all know, that we can suffer for what we store up in our personality. It is part of preparation for old age to keep the portals of the heart and store the key with Christ. The Prodigal Son brought more than his rags home from the piggery. Was he a lad from Galilee, seduced by the flashy glamour of some Decapolis city across the lake, finding that 'this is not what that was', and stumbling home in time for restoration, as I urged the boy in Leicester Square to do? Suppose he spent his money in Gerasa, a great Greek town, as the ruins of Jerash show. Could he ever quite empty his person of sights, sounds, events, put together in those back streets? His patrimony was all gone, and that was not restored to him.

Therein is tragedy. John Masefield has a vivid poem about an aged villain who had sailed once in a pirate's crew. Sharp in his memory was a day when, as the sun dipped red, their ship came in under topsails to a remote deserted bay. Here the gang unloaded its loot. In 'a half-score battered chests' they carried their gold and silver through the marshes, enough to 'make a beggar-man as rich as Lima Town'. There were 'gold doubloons, and double moidores, louis d'ors and portagues. . . .' They buried it as the moon came up, blazed the tree and sailed away. And now the sodden old wreck, begging in the wet street, is 'the last alive that knows it'. He's 'old and nearly blind, and an old man's past's a strange thing for it never leaves his mind'.

> *And I go singing, fiddling,*
> *old and starved and in despair,*
> *And I know where all that gold is hid,*
> *if I were only there.*

Yes, if one could go back in a shattered life and find one special place, one forking of the path, one hour of mis-choice. . . . But it cannot always be done. . . . I saw another sight on that same occasion, as I tried to fill in an idle day in London. I had lunch at the Olde Cheshire Cheese, and wished I had not. I was alone, and on other days I had enjoyed the old seat under Sam Johnson's picture, because there was a loved one, Kathleen, my wife, with me. In my nostalgic return, I had miscalculated that lack. I was on my way to St Paul's, for a privilege I have as an OBE is to go free to the crypt. I like to do so, for the Order's chapel is there, and I pray for my dear family and give thanks for past joys, vanished though many of them may be. The 'Dreamtime' of the Australian aborigines, haunts the evening of our day.

It was, as I said, a perfect day, and on a wooden bench asleep at the bottom of Ludgate Hill I saw him. A battered remnant of a hat had slipped from his red stubbled face. He wore a World War One trench coat, stiff and black with the grease and dirt of years. A filthy shirt without a collar was open at his thin neck. His boots were broken, his hand clutched a torn bundle of old newspapers, his covering or pillow for the night. Beside him was a plastic bag containing all he owned, and someone, in a gush of pity, had bought a packet of ham sandwiches and placed them, incongruously immaculate, on the plastic bag. It was a spectacle for tears.

What had gone wrong? He had never intended this in his bright youth. Somewhere he had chosen wrongly. The morning paper said they had plucked the remains of twenty-six others like him from the nearby river. Some dire choice lay somewhere behind, some failure to prepare, to use the fragile years, to build a base for age. It all makes my point, does it not? To grow old is a process for which, in the total stretch and tract of life we must prepare, husbanding resource and cherishing the years. Says Saul Kane in the same Masefield:

> *I wondered then why life should be,*
> *And what would then become of me,*
> *When youth and health and strength were gone*
> *And cold old age came creeping on.*

Saul found a path back in Masefield's story. The old man on the bench by the railway bridge did not. As Vergil said: 'There are the tears of things.'

It need not be, no, it need not be. The preparation for old age must begin in youth. Old age can come in middle life, as the swagman on the 'wallaby track' said in the Australian bush ballad, and the heaviest burden of old age must be a stock and stack of agonised regrets. But to end this chapter less sombrely let us look at Oliver Wendell Holmes who himself lived fruitfully and creatively until eighty-five. When Julia Ward Howe, who wrote 'The Battle Hymn of the Republic', was seventy in 1879, Holmes remarked: 'To be seventy years young is sometimes to be far more cheerful than to be forty years old.' Julia lived until 1910. Perhaps the secret was her own line in the hymn: 'Be swift my soul to follow him be jubilant my feet.'

I do not know how old (or young) Holmes himself was when he wrote the verse:

> *Call him not old whose visionary brain*
> *Holds o'er the past its undivided reign*
> *For him in vain the envious seasons roll*
> *Who bears eternal summer in his soul.*

It seems as if there is some principle, applicable in this life as in eternity in the strange verse of the Apocalypse: 'He that is unjust, let him be unjust still: and he which is filthy, let him be filthy still: and he that is righteous, let him be righteous still: and he that is holy, let him be holy still.'

In life's complete pattern we cannot be too early in weaving in the right threads. . . . Nor have I forgotten what I said to the ruined boy in Leicester Square. By the grace of God there is a way back, but the further the path is left behind the more difficult it is to penetrate the jungle which closes in upon us. There is no doubt hope while life abides. We can, by God's miracle, be 'born again' at any age, but how infinitely better it is to see the reality of life in time, to observe the laws of body, mind and spirit and never to end in Leicester Square and on Ludgate Hill.

The Preacher, therefore, was right: the road to old age, if not to a happy or tranquil old age at least to an honourable one, begins from the first consciousness of life, from youth's first rejoicing. 'Remember', the passage begins. We need to do so . . . 'remember your creator, in the days of your youth. . . .'

Chapter Three

'. . . IT NEVER LEAVES HIS MIND'

I must speak next about memory, its peril and its power. The ancient scoundrel, fiddling in the city street, was right: 'An old man's past's a strange thing, for it never leaves his mind.' Memory is a major concern of life's evening. It is, in truth, 'the warden of the brain', and capriciously, it seems, sometimes unlocks the mind's remotest cells 'hung with the ragged arras of the past. . . .' Everything appears to be imprisoned somewhere there within, too often the years' debris, and at some odd turn of circumstance or quirk of thought, can be sped complete to the forefront of consciousness.

Edward Ernest Bowen lived from 1836 to 1901, the whole of the Great Queen's reign. At what period of his life he wrote his lamentable song for Harrow school seems not to be recorded. But how wrong he was about 'forty years on'. The 'little victims', to quote another poet of another public school, would be by then in the prime of life and the mind's activity and, looking back, would most certainly not 'forgetfully wonder what they were like at their work and their play'.

I am certainly not alone in remembering in the minutest detail scenes from my very earliest childhood, especially words which hurt me, the cruel taunt of a classmate, the sneer of a teacher. We left Birmingham for my father's bold move to 'the colonies', in the week of my sixth birthday, but I remember much of the grey old Midland city – my father, waiting at the school gate in Handsworth, one leg astride his bicycle with its pillion seat for me, the star-shaped depressions punched in the paving stones of our footpath, to hold the feet in slippery weather, Peter Pan stepping through a stage window at a 'pantomine'. Of the vast adventure of migrating to New Zealand, I hold scenes from the Tilbury dockside to the Three Kings in the spray-lashed sunrise, sharp and coloured in the memory.

I have heard it said that those who hold thus in clear recall the more distant years, find commonly that scenes of middle life and later years tend to blend and blur. I have certainly not found it so. The past spins out and accumulates behind, and whatever future lies ahead grows invisibly shorter as that travelling point we call the present moves along the thread of time, but I have not found memory dimmed for any portion or year of what has been a full life. I do sometimes feel conscious of a beneficent machinery at work lightly, too lightly, erasing the recollection of more distant unhappy events, but such a mechanism, I think, requires an environment of domestic wellbeing in which to function well, and it has been a part of my life's blessedness, until most recent years, to have a home which was a refuge from all storm, and a fellowship which could hardly have been more richly complete. Kathleen died, as I told in the book I wrote about her, four long years ago.

It is with the shattering of such bliss, a treasure more fragile as the years go by, that memory becomes a burden to be borne, and old age must brace itself for battle. Felicia Hemans who, for all the brevity of her forty-two years of life, knew much irremediable sorrow, wrote: 'Though the past haunts me like a spirit, I do not ask to forget.' The words express the dilemma well. Sorrow remembered is sorrow still, and sorrow's crown of sorrow is remembering happier things (I strongly suspect I am half-quoting there). But let those who think they offer stricken old age comfort when they murmur 'But you have your memories', bear also in mind how sharp a shaft they are launching.

I have climbed no pulpit with these notes on age. What I am here writing will in due course be a book and, if so, it must be truth. Our university has an oddly named department – that of Continuing Education – in which (my only remaining contact with Alma Mater) I talk at times on ancient history. Life is 'continuing education', sometimes in a stern classroom. Much of what I here say was not known in its clarity to me until a long four years ago. But I tell the truth as the truth has come to me, and I agree with the poetess, as forgotten now as her sad verse is, that, for all the cost, you would not have memory chilled. It may mar the year with remembered dates, it may make it impossible to visit some places, to read some books again, but memory is life, and life must be held undiminished and complete, and that is why, if it were available, I would not accept the medicine for which Macbeth pleaded which can

> *Pluck from the memory a rooted sorrow,*
> *Raze out the written troubles of the brain*
> *And with some sweet oblivious antidote*
> *Cleanse the stuffed bosom of that perilous stuff*
> *Which weighs upon the heart. . . .*

We cannot, for all that, pause there, or life would be difficult to face. Life must be faced with courage and with faith, for as many years as God decrees. Memory must be disciplined and made to serve. If it cannot be purged of pain it must be freed from unnecessary pain. If there is no medicine of Macbeth's prescription, there is in God a therapy for the sicknesses of memory, especially those which assail the lonely mind in a now silent house, memories, not of grief, but born of some metabolite of grief, which should find 'oblivious antidote'.

'Youth is a blunder,' said Disraeli, 'manhood a struggle, old age is a regret.' Disraeli was right only about manhood which is indeed a fight for a man with a faith, a God and a conscience. About old age he then knew nothing. He wrote *Coningsby* in 1844 at the age of forty. He lived until 1881. Old age, of course, can be a regret and perhaps he later found it so. There can be regret for opportunities missed, deeds not done which should have been done, wrong choices made, for life after all is choice more than chance. Thousands 'know where all that gold is hid, if only they were there'. But regret for that which time has placed beyond remedy is useless, and it is best not to repine.

Especially, and so frequently after an agonising bereavement, come suddenly, poignantly, recollections of some hasty word, some act of insensitivity, of thoughtlessness which should have been avoided. They bear a load of self-reproach and should most resolutely be put aside. The one who caused hurt, if such earthly memories continue where the departed live (and we do not know) has been abundantly forgiven. Nor does repentance include a penitential debt, or demand daily renewal. 'I will remember their sin no more,' says God, and if God can forget a wrong we have done, by what right or folly should we remember? If such sick thoughts persist, draw some good from them. Let them soften the heart.

True, there befalls us at times battle fatigue and weariness of mind which open those closed doors in our person. The mind (or is it the mind's tool and instrument, the brain itself?) cannot be always controlled and made to serve. It is in precisely that way that we differ from the beast which, for all the speed and precision of his body's responses, acts and reacts according to the programming of its brain and nervous reticulation. We possess that which we call the soul, the spirit, which is the Something Else which makes us human.

That is why it is easier to give directions about what to do with the phenomena of memory than to put the process to work. We cannot always slam and bolt those doors. Could Paul, who bade the Philippians' forget those things which are behind', ever forget Stephen's face on that steep slope outside the gate above the dry Kidron valley? Could he be ever sure that there would not rise before his inner eye the awful picture of the barearmed dignitaries picking up the jagged stones and dashing them into the bloodied features of a man, the pile of garments at his own feet . . . ? Could he? He had sought to forget in a frenzy of persecuting activity, and had only added to the pictures in his brain the stricken faces of men and women whom he had tormented. . . .

And yet he meant what he wrote to Philippi, how he made it his aim to forget the forgiven evil of the past. He was under house arrest in Rome, daily sentries supplied by the Praetorian Guard. It was in those hideous years in which the bronze-bearded young Nero had just begun his criminal career, unchecked now by Seneca and Burrus, the former his old tutor, the other the Praetorians' commander. Rome was racing-mad, from the sadistic young prince down to the dregs of the city mob. Paul could catch the distant roar of the crowd in the Circus Maximus, and hear the tales of the soldiers changing guard. He would hear horrifying stories of disaster, mangling and death on the course. Hence the disguised imagery in the passage of the Philippian letter quoted. He had more than once used metaphor and simile from the Greek games. In this, I think, he referred to the fearsome Roman chariot race.

I shall translate it: 'Not that I have already won the prize, or already reached perfection, but I press on, that I may lay firm hands on that for which the Lord laid firm hands on me. Brothers, I do not count myself to have done this, but this one thing I do – forgetting the things behind, and stretching out to those which are before, I make for the mark, the prize of the upward calling of God in Christ Jesus . . .'

He was writing to a Roman colony from Rome itself, hot with the fever of competition between the rival racing colours. Such a race as that which forms the substance of Paul's figure is described well in the novel *Ben Hur*. The charioteer stood on a tiny platform set over a sturdy axle and large wheels. His knees were pressed against a curved front-guard, his thighs sharply flexed. He bent forward from the waist, stretching out with body, arms and clutching hands over the back of his four-horse team. This is what Paul must mean by 'stretching out to the things before'. The reins were wound round his body, and braced on the reins the body formed a taut, extended spring. It can easily be seen how completely the charioteer was at the mercy of his team's sure feet and his own precise driving skill. Euripides, the great Athenian tragedian, describes how Hippolytus, in such a drive, fell and was killed. Much nearer to Paul's own day the Roman poet Ovid tells of a similar disaster. In his tense preoccupation the driver dare not cast a glance at the things behind. The roaring crowd, yelling praise or blame, the racing of his rivals, all else had to be forgotten. The touch of another's wheel, a grazing of the longitudinal wall down the centre, round which the chariots tore, seeking the inner lane and a sharp turn, had perforce to be forgotten. One object alone could fill the driver's vision, the point to which he drove on each lap. Four balls were uplifted on one end of the central wall, four 'dolphins' at the other. One was taken down at the end of each lap.

How intense was Paul's figure of speech, and what a comment on easy-going religion the picture of life as he saw it! He tried to forget uproar in synagogue and Sanhedrin, stones thrown at Lystra, the market mob in Thessalonica, the ramshackle prison in Philippi, the court in Corinth, the scorn of the Epicureans, his own wrongdoings. Did he? Did he forget Stephen? Clearly not. Nor did he forget persecution in Damascus, nor pain in the towns of central Asia Minor. Among the last words he wrote as his second imprisonment slid towards his martyrdom were: 'You are fully aware,' he says to Timothy, 'of what I teach, the way I live, my purpose, faith, endurance, love, patience, persecutions, and sufferings which came unto me at Antioch, Iconium, and Lystra; what persecutions I endured.'

Was Paul, then, defeated, or coveting some impossible oblivion? He was too sane a man for that. He saw life whole, and knew that the past was a part of it. He would undoubtedly recommend to any forgiven man that he should try to cast off the agony of purged misdeeds. A Christian need cherish no guilt complex, carry no debilitating remorse for what Christ has borne for him and 'nailed to his cross'. He is free to forgive himself for the sins which God has forgiven. He may pray: 'Lord make me deaf and dumb and blind, to all the things that are behind . . .' But he should certainly not forget the pit from which he was dug.

What then was Paul saying? In the context of what he wrote to Philippi he was bidding us regard the prize and not the onlooker. In his first letter Peter keeps telling the Christians of the churches to which he wrote in northern Asia Minor, so to live that the lies current about them should be shown for lies. There are few Christians, especially those in the public eye, who have not experienced the shock of pain in confrontation with falsehoods written or spoken wantonly about them. A university press sent me the other day a letter written scurrilously by a very minor poet twenty-nine years ago about me, asking for my permission to include it in a collection of the person's works. It haunted me for days. I hate lies, as David, the psalmist, did. But such matters are best forgotten and left in the mire which engendered them.

Concentrate, Paul is saying, on the future, the rest of the race, not on what taught you how to drive the chariot. Christ can fill the future with fellowship and purpose. To be sure there are circuits in our damaged brains which can be reanimated by satanically contrived patterns of circumstances, and to stop them in their course may indeed call for discipline and effort, penetrated by prayer. That is part of the battle of life. Battles can be stubborn conflict, and part of a long campaign. That, too, is to be expected. Giving due weight to the linear force of the Greek present imperative in Romans 12:2, we can translate: 'Press on with the transformation which came with the renewing of your minds, and find out in practice what that good, acceptable and perfect will of God is.'

The sum of it is, then, that memory has its place. For myself I treasure its pain. I never visit the village supermarket without looking up the adjacent stairs to the hairdresser's salon where, in her last brave effort to carry on with life, Kathleen fell and lay, a few days before she limped out of my life to spend the last weeks in the medical care of her son and the gracious nursing of his dear wife. I pause, pray for courage, and look at those half dozen top stairs. It has become a small homage, the sanctifying and purifying pain of which I would not deny myself. Memory has its place, did I say? It is part of life, and the diminishing span of years ahead of me must increasingly be fed by it. Once hurt, a beast may fear the source of that which hurt him. It is a programmed reaction. Man can take hold of that which hurt him and force himself with God's aid to make it serve him.

Paul did that. His Philippian word picture meant no more. Like a parable, his meaning must be read within its context, and not twisted and tormented into significance beyond its intention. Did he not say in writing to the Roman Christians, showing precisely how all life is one: 'We rejoice in our sufferings because we know that suffering produces perseverance, perseverance character, and character hope . . . '? He would postulate the same of joyous experience, for life is not unbroken darkness for all the lengthening of the shadows in our latter years. And the link which binds this process together into one strong sequence is memory.

Let us then treasure it, but not expect it to be freed from pain. Time does not heal, but it draws the edges of the grievous wound precariously together, not sufficiently to risk mishandling, but enough to promote some calm in public, and that state the wounded must attain. Job's 'comforters', whose seven days' quiet vigil on the ash heap is sometimes quite forgotten, ended with impatience and reproach which provoked divine displeasure. We cannot expect a weary world to endure another's grief too long. Sorrow becomes a private ordeal which must somehow be transmuted into good.

That is why I still live in this house where I write, on the hill by the forest's edge. It is alive with remembered words. Every corner quivers with the touch of a vanished hand. I have not removed her chair from the great front window where we looked together across the city to the blue blade of the Waitemata and the line of the Pacific, the mauve of the Moehau Range and the lifted peak of the mysterious Rangitoto, nor her chair opposite mine by the library fire, alight again for the third winter as autumn darkens into chilly days. I can see her leap from it as the telephone sounded in case it was her son, ringing from Dunedin, eight hundred miles away, with some news, perhaps of examination results. I remember finding a verse once many years before the Great Sorrow fell on me. I was, for some reason, alone in the house, and the lines drove a dart of apprehension to my heart. They came from Charles Hamilton Aidé, a poet otherwise unknown to me. They ran:

38

> *I sit beside my lonely fire*
> *And pray for wisdom yet –*
> *For calmness to remember,*
> *Or courage to forget.*

I will have none of forgetting. Wisdom and calmness I strive for but do not expect I shall ever open the door without hearing a quick foot on the stair.

I talk to her, but I do guard against living in a world of phantasy. In his copy of Aristophanes which he read as a Classics student at Cambridge, poor Rupert Brooke underscored a line: 'The dead cannot hear you, though you call them thrice.' He was alluding to the Greek practice of calling the dead man's name three times before the pyre was set ablaze. Both poets wrote far outside my context of a Christian faith, but no part of scripture opens the way for any communication with those who have left us, in spite of the words in the hymn about 'blessed, sweet communion with those whose rest is won'. We cannot remotely imagine heaven, and bliss would surely be diminished if our departed loved ones could agonise over our battle.

I know that she would communicate with me were such a fellowship allowed, but I have no consciousness that she is by my side. Indeed, the thought is perhaps a dangerous one. My mind rejects it. On the other hand, God, who suffers with his servants, may in his mercy offer some mystic comfort, which the guarded intellect of an 'academic' can look upon with a sort of wondering hope. Perhaps I dare share one such experience, without dogmatism or delusion, and with a plea not to misunderstand.

Last month I spent a fortnight in Australia, where I managed a huge programme of speaking – radio, schools, theological colleges, churches. I went in haste to Melbourne and Ballarat, and circumstances imposed an eighty-mile dash to the second town where I spoke at seven p.m., though I left Sydney on the four-fifteen plane. To watch the kilometre posts flick by was hair-raising, but I was glad to have the journey over because I went there, I mean we both went there, four years ago, when the anxiety was closing in. I did not want to journey from Melbourne to the Bible Society dinner in the old gold-mining town again. . . . After the function a man approached me and said: 'My mother died on the same day as your wife. I am here as a Christian because of your book.' I went back to Melbourne afterwards, and as the broad horizon of the city's lights grew clearer from every rise on that rolling sheep country, I felt a lifting of a load and a thankfulness which filled my inner being.

Observe that I begged not to be misconstrued. I do not say that a loved one went ahead to Ballarat (the word is aboriginal for 'a resting place') but is it within the orbit of God's loving kindness that a message came from him which only faith in God can risk interpreting? I have hesitated to record the story for fear of misleading. I have too many recollections of 'testimonies', calculated only to make their hearers feel deprived, inferior and desperate, to risk a chance of stirring spurious hopes, the seeking of 'signs', or any presumptuous mishandling of another's inner life, or to join any band of sons of Eliphaz. Read the fourth and fifteenth chapters of Job and hear the first of the sufferer's friends. The man had once a remarkable mystic experience. In a strange vision of the night Eliphaz had been made aware of another world of being, a spirit brushing his very face and giving voice. He had been singled out, he implies, for a mystical message. He has no other truth to utter. His religion is familiar dogma and memorised texts. His 'great experience' is his religion, the core of his faith, the basis of all spiritual diagnosis. Such people are lame helpers, a source of despair for the afflicted.

Not of such sort are the 'visions' of the prophet Joel which the apostle Peter quoted in the first words of his Pentecost sermon: '. . . your young men shall see visions and your old men shall dream dreams . . .' This is an oracle, which is not the mere parallelism of Hebrew poetry. Youth has a short past, and in God has sanguine hopes and bright plans for the future. They seek, in the ardour of new faith, to grasp the years to be, to expect much, and not infrequently see their imagination accepted of God and transformed into truth by life's touch. Old men have a long past and a short future. Their expectation is built of life's experience and tempered memory. Dreams are built of the stored recollections of the years as all dreams tend to be. It is a pity we do not know what experience of Christ formed the dream of Pilate's wife. It might illustrate the case. But in the oracle, Joel speaks of sanctifying and dynamic memory. It should be the sum of all our striving so to deal with all that lies behind. So can memory be woven into the pattern which God and good can weave for all of us.

In conclusion: In these three chapters I have written much of the past. I do so more and more as a correspondent peevishly informed me, referring to the newspaper column which I have achieved once a week for almost forty-one years. The answer is simple. The past lengthens. I can write little, with the integrity I cherish, of the future, for all the readers and the popularity which such adventuring can bring to those who feed man's hunger for the unknown.

The past accumulates, and that is true of my critic, of me and 'Uncle Tom Cobleigh and all'. The past contains the only wealth which cannot be filched from us. It can be reviewed, savoured, examined for its truth, purged of its folly, and sometimes healed of its pain. It can be fused, in a blessed amalgam, into the future, provided that balance between remembering and forgetting, which has been our theme, is achieved.

Let us then have an eye to that immensely powerful point which we call the present, with its awesome and explosive possibilities. Marcus Aurelius, the philosopher emperor, musing by lamplight in the chill camps by the Danube, as he strove to prop that sadly sagging frontier, wrote among his meditations: 'Every man's life lies within the present. The future is uncertain.'

How many times has some such sage remark warned us to use memory to cleanse today. Hear Blaise Pascal, that writer of polished French, and founder of so much polished thought. 'The present,' he said three centuries ago, 'is never our final object. Past and present we use as our means. The future is our end.' And Pip, in Dickens's *Great Expectations*, speaking of a day which 'wrought great changes' in him: 'Pause you who read this,' wrote Dickens, moralising more like Thackeray than his usual self, 'and think for a moment of the long chain of iron or gold, of thorns or flowers, that would never have bound you but for the formation of the first link on one memorable day . . . tomorrow looked me more steadily in the face than I could look at it.'

That is why we must be careful with that which we allow into life and mind at any moment. Today's thought and experience will be tomorrow's memory. And we should remember what challenges, purges, encourages. Memory is a precious possession.

Chapter Four

'BY THE SWEAT OF THY BROW . . .'

I saw Ithaca once, indomitable, enduring old Ulysses' island, and it stays, etched in black and silver, on my mind. I was on a Greek ship racing through the Ithaca Channel as the full moon rose suddenly over the jagged crouching mass of the high island, and sped a beam of golden light towards us across the dark water. To that hunched mass of barren crags, his 'grey spirit yearning with desire', came the hero Ulysses, back after years of battle and adventuring up and down the storied seas.

He had nothing to do that his pedestrian son Telemachus could not do, to 'mete and dole out laws' for a peasantry 'that hoard, and sleep and feed. . . .' He could not rest from a life's labours. He wanted to shine in use. A sail puffing in the breeze, where the lights began to twinkle on the seashore, where the full moon, as I saw it that night, climbed, set him longing. He felt himself grasping for the brief remainder of life. I found myself quoting as the ship's spearhead of waves wrinkled the moonlight. I found the poem, as I have written already, in the fifth form, and have known it by heart ever since:

> *Old age hath yet his honour and his toil;*
> *Death closes all; but something ere the end,*
> *Some work of noble note, may yet be done*
> ....
>
> *Tho' much is taken, much abides; and tho'*
> *We are not now that strength which in old days*

> *Moved earth and heaven, that which we are, we are,*
> *One equal temper of heroic hearts,*
> *Made weak by time and fate, but strong in will,*
> *To strive, to seek, to find, and not to yield.*

It will easily be guessed, if the chapter title did not give an ample warning, that now my theme is work, the one force and substance which can make the future full and rich. We have looked long at the past, and it was inevitable that memory should do so. We have paused over the Bible's twin exhortations to remember and to forget. We looked last at the immense significance of the present, and those agate points of choice which tilt life's balance. We look now at the future, and it lies in two parts strangely joined and continuous.

There is first that unimaginable world in which, if Christ be risen, we shall find our being. That mode of living will not be one endless tract of idleness. John Greenleaf Whittier, the tender American poet, put that well in his piece about the dying Piero Luca, the 'grey porter of the Pitti wall'. 'Your work is done,' said the monk beside him.

> *No toil, no tears, no sorrow for the lost*
> *Shall mar the perfect bliss. Thou shalt sit down*
> *And wear a golden crown. . . .*
> *For ever and for ever.*

Piero groaned. A golden crown would be too heavy for his grey old head. He had no wish to 'sit among the lazy saints'. Horrified, the monk fled such blasphemy, but a Presence by him gave assurance that his 'work below should be his work above'.

A beautifully told story, by the Quaker writer of 'Dear Lord and Father of Mankind' (who lived to eighty-five years) and a parable of truth. Heaven cannot be everlasting unemployment. Did not Christ say: 'My father is at work until this very moment and so am I,' in no way contradicting what the Creation story says about God resting on the seventh day. The process of Creation in a wider sense is eternal, but Eternity, in the thought and language of earth, lies beyond what 'we mortals', as Aslan said to the children in C. S. Lewis's last Narnia book, 'call Death'. That glorious creativity belongs to another world of being though, to be sure, that world is continuous and contiguous with this. The one who commits himself to Christ is absorbed into a long sequence of life, which began with man's beginning, and continues. To be thus absorbed is to have what John calls 'eternal life'.

Let us then go back to Eden for there is a thread there that runs all through life, and must remain unbroken 'between the sunset and the stars'. There was no idleness envisaged in the Garden. That unspoiled and unpolluted place was a beginning, as the very name of Genesis implies. An awesome sequence was there inaugurated in which man was to become a partner in creation with his Maker. He was put in the Garden 'to serve and to keep it', preserve its excellence, to promote its fruitfulness. In spite of the shyness of translators, the Hebrew text does say 'serve'. Work was not the penalty of the Fall, it was the first command to man.

Man was 'given dominion' over a lovely planet, its flora and its fauna, and those who blame the Judaeo-Christian work ethic for the despoiling, ravaging, looting and poisoning of the globe, simply do not understand what a pure and sinless 'dominion' means. Man was not to rule for himself, to consume, to take. He was to rule for that which was given into his charge and keeping, and give equally and to feed.

'No man safely rules,' said Thomas à Kempis, 'but he who has learned gladly to obey.' The Vast Intelligence which is God could have conditioned and programmed man so that he would have obeyed without the involvement of his will, but God was creating not a magnificent computer but a being endowed with free will, built, as the great statement has it, 'in his image', to be his partner in the timeless process of creation. Man can still visibly conform to that commission, producing predictable results, or he can, with the inevitable consequence, break what Isaiah in that sombre twenty-fourth chapter, calls 'the everlasting covenant'.

45

The commission is not withdrawn or cancelled with the onset of old age, and a key is here to usefulness. Glad work was one of the proferred privileges of humanity. Work, looked upon only as a weary burden to be shed, a chore to be diminished and avoided, came only with disobedience and man's determination to follow his own wilful path. And that is why work takes its colour from the acceptance or repudiation of God's plan. Eden, then, was an apprentice-ship. It was surely God's intention to give man, in his own good time, the knowledge he snatched prematurely from the tree. Is not that a still visible and primal fault of man, to lay hold in self-will with spoiling hands on what God will in the end give, interfused with his beneficence? Read again Bunyan's perceptive picture in the Interpreter's House of Passion and Patience.

Was God defeated, was God taken by surprise? We cannot give a clear answer to these deeper questions in the story. We can do no more than see the nearward parts, and find them true to life. God seems, in a manner beyond finite comprehension, to move within the actual and the poten-tial, and we do well to think and act within the ambit of comprehension. Nor, in these musings on old age, is more here before us than how worthily to face the final chapter, and enjoy the fulfilling task of work.

God certainly was not creating an immortal gardener. He had made a wondrous being when he breathed into the glorious creature 'the breath of life', a man, with mind, emotions, a being able to hold converse with him, to grow, to discover, to move in tune with the world's beauty. Hence the obtuseness of G. B. Shaw's irritating play *Back to Methuselah*. Adam appears in the opening scene brooding over his doom – to live for ever. 'The horror,' he complains, 'of having to be with myself for ever. I want to be different, to be better, to begin and begin again, to shed my task as a snake sheds its skin. . . . If only there may be an end one day. If only the care of this terrible garden could pass on to another gardener. I am not strong enough to bear eternity.'

Eternal, unchanging sameness no one could bear. C. S. Lewis is more perceptive in his lovely Eden, Perelandra. His Adam and Eve live a life of breathless new discovery.

46

They have before them a task of astonishing significance. Shaw's Adam was looking at some limitless extension of time, in which, as Mercury threatened Prometheus in Shelley's strange play,

> *the reluctant mind*
> *Flags wearily in its unending flight,*
> *Till it sinks, dizzy, blind, lost, shelterless.*

That, indeed, might be doom, but such long-drawn ages are not what the Word calls 'eternal life'. That boon is a quality of living, not a stretch of time to be measured by never-pausing clocks or calendars. It is the life of God himself, and work is its mode of self-expression and activity. That is how it comes about that evil poisons work, and degrade it into the boredom which man bears today. Work is a lovesome thing, a joyous exercise, and it will only be by a rediscovery of that element in labour, that man will, if he does so in time, conquer the deserts which encircle the globe. The victory recedes while clever hands and brains devote their powers to machines of massacre, and impatient labour turns from all toilsome tasks. Such is 'the Curse'.

Consider what man has achieved and ask if more fragments of what once was are not to be found in man's remote endeavour much more clearly sometimes than is manifest today. Consider the chipping of a flint, the boring of a hole for a haft in a shaped piece of basaltic stone. . . . I have by me for a paper weight an axe-head of stone shaped and smoothed in Stone Age Antrim. Its every curve is beautiful. Whoever smoothed and honed it spent weeks on the task. Not a line in it, whichever way it is turned, fails to charm with its purity. The axe-maker wanted to do more than make a tool. So did the lamp-maker who, in similar black stone, when Hiram was king of Tyre, hollowed out a shapely tiny lamp on which can still be seen the blackening of the burnt oil. For joy in his work, infinitely complicated, as he hollowed the stone, he cut a pattern to decorate the top. It was buried with its owner over three millennia ago, outside the Phoenician town, and now is by me.

The point I want to make is that beauty is beyond utility. It seems part of instinct to create. Art is man's alone. It is part of the marred image of God, this urge to create beauty for beauty's own sake, in form, sound and colour, and so render the deeper experiences of life. It is open still, as it was in Eden, to be one of a partnership. And man can still ruin old age by opting instead for self, by shunning the challenge, and ceasing to work. That is not to say that man, like Shaw's Adam, is dismally fated to stumble on under the load of a stupefying task.

On the contrary it is to realign life with life's original purpose. Work only sours and displeases if it is regarded as anything less. This is not to deny unsympathetically that, in society as man has built it, there is still much toil in which it is difficult to see a creative feature. This country, like some others, has an annual holiday celebrating a victory over work, called Labour Day. A political party also claims the name, and justification can be found in the word, if it means that burdens too heavy to be fairly borne can be laid upon manual labourers, for all the coming of machines.

I think of a man named Turchey. When my father, following his romantic dream of 'farming in the colonies', bought his hungry acres in the valley yonder, he had a raupo swamp to drain, a tiny fragment of which still remains beside a suburban road to remind me, when I pass by, of valiant Mr Turchey. In our day, it was deep and sinister, brown with rotted rush and flax. The labourer arrived with no more than a shiny spade. He waded in at one end, and in a few days had all the eight or nine chains of malodorous bog cut into a deep, firm trench, running with clear, free water. He had no waders or gumboots. He was self-employed, took a generous wage in the real currency of those far days, and trudged off home.

There was labour indeed, and the thought of that overworked man makes me thankful for digging machines. The human frame should not be so tormented. A man should not be called upon to wear out joints and muscles so damagingly. And no doubt life still has its many corners where men and women are called upon to wrench their bodies thus. Mr Turchey was working for a home, his amily, some simple ambition beyond the day's dire effort, but he could not be expected to enjoy such work for its own sake. Nor was such the shape of Eden.

Certainly there is other labour besides that of the flesh and bones. There is the less physically stressful toil of delicate fingers, those of the weary surgeon, the maker of pottery, the creator of music. There is the sweat of the brain, as well as the brow. There are the tiring tensions of the personality, in posts of leadership and administration, teaching, commerce. They are more diffuse. When 'the ploughman homeward plods his weary way', commonly he leaves behind his plough. The labour of the head is perhaps not so easily left upon the desk, or behind the blackboard. No one can be expected to carry on past a fixed age the routine and the unremitting demands of tasks so relentless, and my plea for work as the anodyne of age and all that age contains, imposes no life sentence such as this. The only necessity is that work should not cease, and they are fortunate whose work, like mine, continues its significance and its interests, long past the date of its binding obligations.

It is a pity that there should be any form of toil which has no inbuilt satisfaction of heart and mind. Saul Kane, in Masefield's *Everlasting Mercy*, born anew to decency and real life, saw poetry in the ploughed field, the brown earth rolling and the share biting deep through the bitterness and the ugliness of tangled roots and weed. I agree with the third man in the story about Saint Paul's Cathedral when Wren was building. One man, when asked what he was doing, grumpily replied: 'I am chipping this block of stone.' The second, similarly engaged, said: 'I am cutting this block to fit that corner.' The third said: 'I am helping Sir Christopher Wren to build a cathedral.'

It is that sense of partnership which the world needs. There is a rugged essay of Thomas Carlyle about it. 'Set down a brave Sir Christopher,' he wrote, 'in the middle of black, ruined stoneheaps, red tape officials, idle Nell Gwyn Defenders of the Faith, and see whether he will raise a Paul's Cathedral out of that' – and he went on to speak of masons and hodmen, who cut the stone and lugged the mortar and all the rest. Work is cooperative, and society fails when it ceases to be so. Every great creation is impossible without a working partnership, and it is that consciousness of personal contribution which makes work worth while. It is the loss of it which can make retirement a path into the desert and a track to death. It is the retention of it, or the rediscovery of it, in 'some work of noble note' that gives vitality and significance to age.

Let Carlyle go on. There was rocky wisdom in the man (he lived till the age of eighty-six): 'There is a perennial nobleness in work,' he continued. 'Were he never so benighted, forgetful of his high calling, there is always hope in a man that actually and earnestly works. In Idleness alone there is perpetual despair. Work, never so Mammonish or mean is in communication with Nature. The mere desire to get work done will itself lead more and more to truth. Know what you can work at, and work at it like a Hercules – that ancient demigod of toil. This is the finest 'perk' of all, and one beyond the reach of any taxman hard on the tracks of such privilege.

In such advocacy of continued effort I speak necessarily from my own experience. It has been my fortunate lot to carry forward the chief ingredients of an absorbing career into the evening of life. As a teacher of classical literature language and history, I was naturally a teacher of the Bible which is part of ancient history. As a Christian I was, and am, called upon to share knowledge and conviction. All through life my activity outside and in the classroom ran in the two parallel streams. And in passing let it be insisted that, in any vocation, a Christian must set before himself the need to make his daily work a prime front of his witness.

As far as I have been able this has been my endeavour. It is by the grace of God that, in the work of the Chair of Classics, and the activity which has filled now these thirteen years of retirement, the whole has been happily morticed into one continuity of interest. Most of my more exclusively Christian and biblical writing has, in fact, been done in this later tract of life. Other avenues have widened – radio broadcasting, speaking and lecturing here, in Australia and abroad, journalism, travel and the rest. Journalism editorial and columnist, has been a hobby for more than forty years, having taken its origin during a period of slackened activity in university teaching. Travel was an obligation in academic days under a fine scheme of study and sabbatical leave, and it has continued in the leading of many parties to the Middle East and the Mediterranean. In this task, an absorbing one, I have flown hundreds of thousands of miles. I prize opportunities so novel and so wide.

It has also been blessedly demanding. From my arduous youth, with no aid to ease my way through school and university studies, I have always worked, in all fashions, to the limit of my strength. In fact, as I must have already made clear, such a habit has become an article of my faith. May I add this: In my early years as a young Christian, I discovered a chorus to a hymn in the old *Redemption Hymnal*, which ran:

> *Every power for Jesus,*
> *Heart, and brain, and will,*
> *Worked at highest pressure*
> *Till the pulse be still.*

I took those words as an intimate challenge. In the stumbling, wavering manner of man, I have tried, lifelong, to heed their exhortation. They have often driven me on for yet one more mile or made me lift just one more burden. My wisdom in such living has been more than once questioned, and I know that I have no right to set it before others as an obligation or even as an ideal. I simply know that, for me, such endeavour has carried me forwards on life's more sombre pathways and through grief. It has simplified decision at difficult forks in the road, and been abundantly satisfying. It has emancipated me from idleness. And I know, and sympathise with those who find usefulness in retirement elusive. I can advise only imaginative search and endeavour.

At this point a pause must be made. I want to write of idleness. It is tragic that idleness can be enforced, and denote no fault self-chosen, no Edenic opting out of the Great Partnership. This convulsive age, and society, as man in his self-will has built it, has enforced idleness on some. The pathos of that unfeeling word redundancy chills the human spirit. There is little more agonising than the plight of a boy or girl, eager for life, trained and fitted for a task, who finds themself unwanted on the market, or of a man or woman who has given most of a useful lifetime to a task, who see that task melt in their fingers under some ruthless 'reorganisation' schemed by a system under which men and women can become ciphers as anonymous as the nameless multitudes who piled the stone mountains of the useless pyramids. 'The great world does not want us and we go.' I am neither politician nor economist. I do not know how to deal with such tragedy, save to say that, if a way can be discovered out of it, it is by some other form of work and the courage and the will to search for it.

I like the story of the gruff old soldier who became the emperor, Vespasian. An engineer brought and demonstrated to him an ingenious device for hauling stone, of value as he set out to rebuild Rome after Nero's fire and profligacy. He bought the machine and put it away, remarking that the free labourers of the capital needed a means to earn their bread.

There is, for all that, another sort of idleness which is a matter of reprehensible choice. It is a spiritual malady, Sloth, which the moral theologians of medieval times numbered among the seven deadly sins (the others were Pride, Covetousness, Lust, Envy, Gluttony and Anger). The moralists had a special name for Sloth which is revealing – accidie (pronounced aksidi). It came through Latin from the Greek word akédia, which signifies 'negligence', 'indifference', a state of not caring, a torpor of the whole personality which rejected all the activities of life. It is used once or twice in the Septuagint where, for example, it is translated 'heaviness' in the King James Version at Psalm 119:28. It is 'the spirit of heaviness' of Isaiah 61:3.

The translators render 'grief', 'sorrow', 'trouble', but the King James Version is a better translation, for it contains that symptom of shallow breathing, or the sense of a weight

52

upon the chest, which the old writers had recognised in accidie.

One John Cassian, who died at the age of seventy-five in AD 435, wrote much about it, and even managed to draw a distinction between 'accidie' and 'depression', which may have been medieval hair-splitting, but may have been psychologically acute. The life of a monk in the non-labouring orders, or of a hermit, such as those who, in Cassian's century, thronged the deserts of Egypt, must have demanded much of human nature. Cold, ill-fed, often unhealthy or in pain, the victims of perversely chosen, rather than reprehensibly chosen idleness, those men lived lives of stress, which must have made maladies of the mind endemic in the harshly disciplined religious communities. Mental prostration, born of fasting and stern mortification of the body, must have been common. Sturdy souls, like Thomas à Kempis, resisted such damage, perhaps by writing. Francis was busy at Assisi and also survived, but more went down in melancholic depression, and were overwhelmed by guilt over the commission of cardinal sin. Such torpor haunts the edges of overwork, and must be recognised in pursuing the regimen of labour such as I may seem to recommend as a therapy for the ills of unemployed old age.

A real accidie, none the less, can still exist outside the area of the mind's pathology. The term was reintroduced into the Christian vocabulary by Francis Paget who was Bishop of Oxford for a decade from 1901. Self-chosen sloth is inevitably, by some inbuilt feature of the human spirit, the path to wretchedness. Plans need to see past the well-earned post-retirement holiday. Such a symbolic severing of the chains is good, a good undone by those foolish enough to haunt the old place of work. The break must be total. Someone once confessed to me that his ambition was to sit, after retirement, in a park and watch the gardeners at work. An hour is enough for that.

The activity which steadies the mind in later years must be happy. It is work, I urge, not grind. At the touch of boredom and flagging interest, stop, preferably by turning to something else. The form of such activity will vary with each person. It must be activity with some promise of continuity, not likely, in its turn, to falter with the years' annual theft of physical vigour. To tramp in hills or woodlands, or to fish the sea, may be good and healthily preoccupying pastimes, but will they last? Physical vigour in the normally healthy may be prolonged beyond the Psalmist's limit, but inevitable diminution comes at last.

Variety may be desirable. Men and women who have worked with their brains, if they have the enviable gift of nimble fingers, should turn to making things, to woodwork, weaving, art. In similar fashion the manual or technical worker can turn to the activities of the mind. There are numberless fields of study and learning, preferably under discipline. Truck drivers and carpenters have qualified for university degrees. But now is the time to leach out the irksome and shed chores. I myself could have continued to teach classics and all connected with that veritable way of life, but I disliked examining and committee work, and loathed driving into town through the increasingly congested streets. I was well rid of that which bothered me.

But all this is common sense. I am musing on the ways and means of ageing, not writing a book of rules for a retirement study course. Given acceptance of the thesis, that work is healthy, that it is a divine provision, and that it is an obligation to link with the very activity of God, the rest will fall into place for those who seek. Keep the body moving while it can. All are not Caleb, but all can listen to him. Keep the arteries of the brain full. They, too, expand with use.

Let the Venerable Bede close the chapter. Bede, first of England's classical scholars, was only sixty-two when he died in AD 735, but that was old age in those bleak centuries. He was all his life at Jarrow in the great school which he founded and where he tirelessly taught and wrote. His total of forty-five books was prodigious for those days with writing as writing then was. 'Learn with what speed you may,' he begged his 'boys' as he felt his last sickness coming. 'I know not how long I will last.' His final task was the translation of John's Gospel, the work of the aged apostle. The last dawn came. 'There is still a chapter wanting,' said the scribe, 'but it is hard for you to question yourself any more.' 'It is easily done,' said the old man. 'Take your pen and write quickly.' 'It is finished now,' said the scribe. 'You speak truth,' said Bede. 'It is finished.' He died as the sun sloped, England's first great Greek scholar, her greatest historian, a founder of English literature. . . . 'Old age has still his honour and his toil. . . .' What a way to end. That should be our hope: 'Every power for Jesus.'

Chapter Five

'THE LAST ENEMY'

This is a difficult chapter to write. In fact this is a second attempt. And why? I read what I had written, and missed something vital in its theme. It was this, I concluded: A gust of fresher air invaded the whole theme of death with the coming into the world of the Christian faith and its risen Christ. The contrast between old and new is striking in Rome. Along the Appian Way are the epitaphs of the pagan dead, cynical, hopeless, bitter, resigned. Down below in the endless galleries of the Catacombs, where lie a multitude of Christian dead, the new hope lives. They sleep 'in Christ', 'in peace'. And so, as I speak of death, I want this to be remembered. We sorrow not as some, said Paul.

I must, in such a book, say something of the end of life, of earth's ultimate experience. 'As the shadows lengthen', in the words of that yearning old hymn, 'over the little landscape of our lives', how can anyone who thinks quite banish the thought of death? – the thought, too, of dying, a different subject to which I must return. Nor need that be a preoccupation only of life's later years. . . .

I have spent this winter evening among my books. They contain the reading of more than half a century. I have read again the dark poetry of the Roman Lucretius, a poet unknown save in the massive beauty of the verse he left behind, sombre verse, as his fear-filled mind fought to convince itself that no horror of judgment and dire retribution lay beyond death. I remember when I first met and read him, as a Classics undergraduate, and recalled my fascinated pity for a tormented soul wrestling with some childhood trauma. 'Therefore death is nothing and concerns us not at all' was his theme, argued with a vehemence which pathetically betrays itself. Lucretius was not, it seems, an old man when he died, but a melancholic suicide, it is my guess. A French psychiatrist, who had Lucretius in his pocket as he fought with the maquis, professes to see, in his six books of verse, the characteristic undulations of such depression. Pondering the Latin text tonight, I picked up again some echoes of my own youth's thinking, the questions I faced on that threshold, and the Christian answers it was my lot to find, and which have ever steadied me. Lucretius is translated. Read Books 3 and 5.

No, there is no decade which has monopoly in such thinking. Alfred Tennyson, the poet who often touches me profoundly, was twenty-one in 1830 when he published his first verse. The third poem in that early collection ends 'all things must die'. He was forty-one when, in 1850, the year he was made poet laureate, he published *In Memoriam* whose noble prologue meant much to my early Christian faith. *In Memoriam* contains the rich harvest of seventeen years of brooding over the death of his young friend Arthur H. Hallam, in Vienna in 1833. Tennyson was to survive Hallam for over sixty years, and was to show in his last poetry a deeper tranquillity than parts of *In Memoriam* bear, but how human that great poem is, how utterly honest and, for that reason, how poignantly real in its message. I have lived with it intimately in recent years, and found great response of spirit, under 'that Shadow feared of man which keeps the keys of all the creeds'. Its sentiments can penetrate the loneliness of a sorrow which aches on and on in spite of surrounding love and unshaken faith, when some words fall tritely, some folk grow weary, and when the world, disliking too long a reminder of mortality, can turn impatient:

> *One writes that 'Other friends remain',*
> *That 'Loss is common to the race' –*
> *And common is the commonplace,*
> *And vacant chaff well-meant for grain. . . .*
> ....

Another answers, 'Let him be,
He loves to make parade of pain,
That with his piping he may gain
The praise that comes to constancy.'

The doubts, the fears, the memories – Tennyson touches them all with the gold of his verse – far more delicately than Milton, when he wrote 'Lycidas' on the death of Edward King, his friend drowned off Anglesey in 1637. That poem did indeed strike a new note in English poetry, but it reads like a brilliant academic exercise beside Tennyson, with no probing of the heart's realities. Milton at the time was only twenty-nine. How old De Quincy was when he confessed that in summer weather he found the thought of death obsessive, I do not know. He speculated that it was due to the sense of infinitude in the skies, measured by the still, piled cumulus, or Nature's exuberance of life which prompted contradictory thought. . . .

It is strange how thought flits and what fragments reach the memory. From De Quincy's curious confession, as I sat with books on the hearthrug, my mind went back to such a day in quiet, high summer half a century ago, when I talked with a friend in a wooded bay on the Manukau Harbour. It is little more than a mile from where I write, as lonely a place in those halcyon days of our youth as it was lovely. There we would sit before our tent behind the beach, and talk as boys talk while the tide rose into the roots of the scarlet cliffside pohutukawas, and receded on the ribbed sand.

Cliff talked that day, with an odd intimacy, of death. He had thought much about it, as he had seen his brothers go to France, and had heard, on their Kentish farm when the wind blew east, the cannonading from the Somme. He was to be my Arthur Hallam, for he died tragically ten years later in Ethiopia, a casualty of Benito Mussolini's ravaging of the land. Some might say he had some premonition of the bandit tribesmen of the Kassi Desert closing in with quivering spears aimed, as he rashly made for Addis Ababa across their wilderness. I think it was just that cold wind of apprehension which brushed the faces of that generation of

58

us who, just too young for involvement, nevertheless felt the horror of the First World War. I remembered the faint chill of that conversation, when the news came and we ceased to hope that the long silence from Africa might have other explanation than the worst. Cliff's sister was my wife. It does illustrate my point that the Last Enemy makes his nearness felt at any stage of life.

It is solemnising to think that whole peoples have lived in the shadow of death, before Christ's light came to break the reign of darkness. They expended treasure and toil to dispel the tears of it. The tragic piles of Egypt's pyramids, built with such expenditure of blood and labour, were designed to keep intact the eviscerated, brainless body of the dead, to be a shell and framework for another life. Yet none of those stone mountains kept their royal occupants safe. Mummification was invented to the same end, and merely preserved some dessicated horrors to stand in the museum cases of another world, mockeries of man's fear of dissolution. It was all elaborate makebelieve. Tutankhamen, gold-wrapped amid his astounding treasures, was as dead as the meanest peasant thrown into a hollowed sand dune with knees drawn up to simulate rebirth.

It made no difference if the dead were burned, like those of Homer's Greeks. 'I had rather live,' said the great Achilles' shade when Odysseus met him on the edge of the last river, 'a servile hind for hire, and eat the bread of a man with scarce enough to wear, than royal empire hold over all the dead.'

It all amounts to a wild, passionate, instinctive rejection of a foul intruder who, at any moment, by blade or fever, can crush or tear from a body, stark with age or vibrant with youth, that which makes it move and feel, and fling it all down to breed corruption. Such hot revolt stems from something which makes us human, each 'a living soul'. That repulsive line in some hymn which speaks of 'Brother Death, which comes to chill our latest breath' is an offence before God. The New Testament names the invader as a foe of all foes. Apart from the empty tomb in the Jerusalem garden, earth would be darkness to the core. There can never be beauty in it whatever the nobility, the quiet

59

courage, the shining faith with which men and women face its hour.

Let us be careful then in the words we use, and in no way let us gild or glamorise the thing itself. . . . In that best-selling novel of the First War, Raymond's *Tell England*, the padre says: 'The only unlovely thing about your friend's death is the way you are taking it.' To my mind, the only lovely thing, the only thing which gave grace and meaning to a boy's bullet-torn body on that bloodstained cliff under Sari Bair *was* a friend's grief. There they lay, six years later when the Graves Commission came in 1921, a swathe of white on the hill, the bones of the last charge, mostly men from my own land and Australia. They died, I know, to quench a tyranny. There was beauty in their sacrifice, but not in death, and those who deal in death and promote the hideous alien thing are the very children of hell.

Christ met death in its ultimate horror. Sensitive in his perfect person beyond any sensitivity we know, he sweated blood of agony as, for us, he faced it. We cannot even imagine his shrinking, but at times some small understanding comes. At Givat Ha-Mitvar, outside Jerusalem, they stumbled on an ossuary in which were crammed the remains of Jehohanan Ha-Gaqol. It was 1968. The pathetic remnants show what crucifixion was. The bones of both forearms were scratched and scored as the young man's tormented body struggled and writhed on the long spikes. The feet had been twisted sideways, and a huge, square nail hammered through the ankles. . . . Christ suffered thus and no one can touch the edge of his anguish of mind and body. This was death. Let there be no minimising of the loathsome thing, this rending apart of soul and body. It is only that Christ defeated it, only because he rose from the dead, that we can face the invader at all.

That is why I do not make light of it, and why I find myself shrinking a little from too casual, too flippant (are those the words I want?) a treatment of the theme. C. S. Lewis, that apostle to the academics, has meant too much to me for me to speak too critically of anything he said. I do, none the less, react against the story, so freely quoted in approval, of his standing in an Oxford street and shouting through cupped hands to the Vanaukens on the other side: 'Christians do not say goodbye.' Perhaps he had the sturdier faith. Perhaps I am woefully wrong. Perhaps my theology needs reaffirming, but Christians, within the only context they know, do say goodbye. Besides, what other word have we? We must turn to French for 'au revoir'. Other people in the High must have heard those words, shot thus through the traffic. Some of them could have thought with a heartstab of the boy in Air Force blue, farewelled at the station on his last leave. Two nights later his riddled plane was spiralling down over the Ruhr. Yes, 'We shall meet again.' But. . . . 'He would have been fifty this year. The children I never had would be grown up.' If Christians do not say goodbye they have no other word. Lewis, of all people, knew that the phrase first meant 'God be with you'. But my point is this. The expression of our faith should not be blatant, should not hurt or in any way incur the charge of insensitivity.

The awe of the unknown covers death. I remember a verse from one of the war poets, like Rupert Brooke pondering Homer on Gallipoli:

> *Was it so hard Achilles,*
> *So very hard to die?*
> *Thou knowest and I know not –*
> *So much the happier I.*

But not for long. Even Lazarus did not tell. But Madame De Stael was right when she said: 'We understand death for the first time when he puts his hand upon one we love.' In sermons, therefore, and in all other contexts of communication, let us walk with proper reverence. This is not to counsel reticence. The Victorians, it is alleged, were over-reticent about sex (though I should rather have reticence than whatever it is we have today) but spoke with no inhibitions about death. We, they say, have reversed the situation. It is not, I think, the tense British tradition of the 'stiff upper lip'. It may be a sort of shame or irritation about an inability to answer, outside a Christian commitment, the fearsome questions death poses. Let us by all means break the silence, but with the utmost gentleness, knowing that there are hinterlands in any person's soul which none can penetrate.

And yet, there is never a time at which our friends need us more desperately or feel more alone. Thus it is that the first unavoidable ordeal of someone brought, intimately and agonisingly, face to face with death, is the funeral. Too many think that this occasion, beyond others, is when they must demonstrate their faith. Let them realise that the bereaved are in a state of shock. They have suffered a paralysing blow. Do not expect them to wear a mask. They are too conscious of the fact that the world is watching how a Christian, especially a Christian of some standing in the community, or, painful to tell, an older Christian, 'will take it'. The watching multitude is wont to say: 'He was broken,' with the faintest note of disapproval; or 'She was so triumphant,' perhaps forgetting the doctor's thoughtful Valium. Nor can they know what their hero or heroine, in obedience to tradition, actually endured, or at what expense that 'victorious' facade was kept firmly standing.

A funeral there must be. Its trial must be faced. It is a tribute owed to the beloved one. It is an opportunity which friends must be given to express their love and fellowship. But, because of the very nature of the gathering, the utmost delicacy and feeling must be exercised. The funeral of a Christian may well be an occasion for a frank forthtelling of a Christian's faith, but it is not every speaker who can be wholly trusted to prepare and speak with propriety. Embarrassment should not be added to sorrow. All proceedings must be conducted with dignity and no assault made on an imprisoned audience, many of whom are present from respect, and not assembled for an evangelistic appeal. The service itself will carry its message.

Forced cheerfulness and laughter, like any faint semblance of exhibitionism, are out of place. The strain on the principal mourners need not be inordinately lengthened. . . . In all this, of course, I am presupposing that the funeral is conducted in a Christian church. I have no suggestions to make for any other form of obsequies. Any warm and understanding minister of Christ would probably counsel in similar fashion.

Those who attend a funeral should also properly conduct themselves. They go to 'weep with those who weep', if they know the bereaved with any intimacy. They should not, therefore, expect their broken friend to stand around, the hearse waiting, for light conversation and recognition afterwards. If opportunity offers be ready with some word of love. Do not expect to be asked to that agonisingly empty house for refreshments afterwards. It is a facility that should not be offered. The custom should be boldly broken. There are limits to human endurance. 'There are the tears of things,' said Vergil, and there should be peace and time given in which to shed them. It is well to remember that your sorrowing friend is never going to forget that date, and will see for the rest of life the end of that casket, the shoulders and locked arms ahead, the faces lining the aisle, the scene outside, wet, fine, mockingly sunny, desolately grey. After a discreet interval, let the cortège go. There is no need for all to follow to a perhaps distant graveside, except for those who, by virtue of intimacy, have some task to perform. Above all, let all involved avoid suggestion that anything such as 'testimony' is at stake. You may be certain that Mary sobbed for her Son. The other Mary certainly wept for Lazarus and found it difficult to get peace in which to do so. Jesus wept before his covered tomb. Leave the appropriate texts to suggest themselves, and the small sermons unspoken.

As the weeks go by, gather round unobtrusively. Never imagine that, because your friend has achieved a deceptive calm, that he has 'got over it', or is 'bearing up wonderfully'. He is not a subject for psychological analysis, much less for a 'spiritual' assessment. Someday, perhaps, you may be called upon to understand more intimately. A little company will help, an opportunity to unload the burden of the heart, at some carefully chosen time, some request for help in which he, she, may rejoin the stream of life. Remember that home is now something other than it was, perhaps a strangely alien place. Encourage speech, but reminisce rather than trade banalities. Do not try to change the subject. Do not imagine that the one who sorrows told you all. There will be hidden corners of the mind which no one else can penetrate, and to which none, perhaps, are admitted. Give advice normally only when asked for it, and do not think, please, that there is a magic word or formula of words that can be somewhere found which will clothe again with life's verdure the ravaged landscape of the years. As with some devastated terrain, Nature must be left to take its time, to grow first the nursling plants, and then the woods.

Be patient with the wounded. They come from a hard battlefield. Let them repeat the story of their strife. Some of them do understand that the world grows weary of bearing others' burdens, and that it is the rarest friend who is always available for comfort. Bear in mind in any fellowship, that the comforters, like those of Job, are also under the scrutiny of God. Had those comforters departed, after sitting with Job wordless for a week, they would have hurt less and learned more. There are those who talk too much and observe too little. That is why Ezekiel, when he visited the exiles in the labour camp on the great Chebar canal, was bidden to 'sit where they sat', for eight days. He did, and was 'astonished' at what he learned.

I am aware that, in speaking thus of the small solemnities and ceremonials of death, I remain within the context of a Western environment. It has its inhibitions and restraints. Some cannot abide the luxury of flowers by which our self-controlled society seeks to express emotion. I myself think they take away some starkness from the scene. Other societies salutarily, it is said, are more open in their grief. There is the Maori 'tangi' or 'wailing' of my own land, the traditional Celtic 'keening' for the dead. We dislike such demonstration, and are at times misunderstood. An Indian student once said to me: 'I wish that the men of your culture knew how to weep.' Alas, I told her, she did not know what wealth of tears I shed – alone. Indeed, though the tension makes the heartstrings crack, we do try to hold a calm exterior before the public, perhaps quite damagingly. Even Americans reveal more, though I shrink from their custom of 'the viewing' with the dead visibly restored to a shocking (so it seems to me) appearance of life. . . . Death? 'It is nothing,' said the poor Roman, Lucretius, whom I quoted. But how enormously real the Last Enemy is astride the path. How glad a thought that Christ defeated him. That must be a note in any funeral.

Chapter Six

LAST ENCOUNTER

We have been squarely facing together in these pages the thought of death. We have sensed 'that ancient awe to know' that we shall one day confront the hour. 'It is appointed unto men once to die. . . .' But wait, someone may interject, after the fashion of Paul's imaginary objector in the opening of the letter to Rome, what of the Second Coming of Christ, for which we are bidden to live in expectation?

And that is a valid interjection, for the Church has not done well so easily to forget what used to be called 'the Blessed Hope'. In the decade which followed the world's direst encounter with death in the First World War, Christ's Second Advent was a common and potent theme of evangelical preaching. Nor is there any doubt that it is part of New Testament doctrine. True, there are apocalyptic passages which are difficult to understand, but there is nothing obscure in the words of the Lord's own promise that he would 'come again'. Those words, too, were reported by the last alive of all the apostles, fully sixty years after they were said. John had not forgotten.

What, then, has so muted the words? The folly, no less, of expositors. The Western mind is obsessed with ordered tabulation, and eschatology had to be reduced to time-tables and sequences. Interpreters split lamentably into virtual sects – 'premillennialist', postmillennialist' and 'amillennialist' – when, in point of fact, no one to my knowledge has ever explained adequately what the millennium is at all. It is one part of the apocalyptic imagery of John's letter to the Asian Churches for which, to date, we have lost the key. It is no disgrace, and it could, indeed, be a becoming humility, to confess that there are some passages of scripture which elude facile explanation. The truth of Christ's coming was thus set aside by many good people, pending more salutary agreement.

And, further to discourage, came the date-fixers, and dogmatic readers of 'the signs of the times'. Disregarding the Lord's own warning that 'ye know neither the day nor the hour', they set out to order a timetable for Almighty God, and find grist for their laborious mills in sources as wide apart as Daniel's later chapters and the measurements of Khufu's Great Pyramid. Can it be wondered that the result was a shyness over what is a scriptural truth? Nor can such a situation be helped by the spate of books which pander to man's desire to penetrate the unknown, and even to turn to profit man's more sombre fears.

That is why, while holding Christ's word in proper reverence, we do well to prepare for life's last solemnity, as Paul bade the volatile Thessalonians prepare. 'He'll find me pickin' cotton when he comes.' And in the mere fact of death there is no cause for apprehension, for what is it that Christ gave supremely to man? By his resurrection he swept aside that mass of morbid ancient fears, and gave assurance that we should have life which would be recognised as life, life in a familiar context of God's love. Apart from that confidence Paul might well say, as he said to the turbulent little congregation on the Corinthian isthmus, 'We are of all men most miserable.'

It should be remembered how enormous, how new, was the gift Christ gave. It is a little daunting to realise that God's faithful in the Old Testament served him without the buoyant lift of a sharp, clear conception of another life in which the uneven balance of this life would find redress. 'Sheol', the place of the dead, shadowy, indiscriminate, sombre, might well be feared.

Two threads may be distinguished in the Psalms. Psalm Six, written, I think, after David's exhausting retreat from Absalom penetrated the dark Jabbok Gorge, sighs: 'In death there is no remembrance of thee: in the grave who shall give thee thanks?' Then in the lovely Psalm Twenty-

Three, if it was written (another guess), when the noble Barzillai, a shepherd-host, restored the psalmist's flagging soul, the cry is 'I will dwell in the house of the Lord for ever.'

Both moods have parallels: 'Shall the dust praise thee? . . . Shall thy lovingkindness be declared in the grave? . . .' Then: 'Thou wilt not leave my soul in hell. . . . My flesh also shall rest in hope. . . . In thy presence is fulness of joy; at thy right hand there are pleasures for evermore. . . . Thou shalt guide me with thy counsel, and afterward receive me to glory.' But there was no assurance until the resurrected Christ walked among men – none. It was he who gave the conviction of continuing personality, and it is that which makes the thought of survival precious and quells the haunting fear.

Where else could it be found? Certainly not in the other beliefs and prevailing philosophies of the day, which range from the hopeless to the fantastic – the chill dissipation of the substance of life into the boundless store of the primeval atoms from which it fortuitously came (thus the Epicureans, and our Lucretius, who was of their school); the reabsorption of the fiery fragment which gives life into the divine flame from which it came (so the Stoics, the other half of Paul's Athenian audience); the rebirth of the disembodied spirit, a divinity briefly entombed in the grave which is the body, in some other shape and form of life (so the followers of Pythagoras) – and so on and on, hopelessly.

Christ's resurrection quenched such surmisings and melancholy expectation. He was still Jesus whom they knew. He was back with them, strangely though he now seemed able to pass in and out of another dimension of life. Death, therefore, awesome fact though it may still remain, has lost its full power over the minds of men. Yes, he was still Jesus, and in that fact lies the knowledge that death does not divide, it reunites. There is no comfort in a commingling of dust, or in a common immersion of what once were sentient beings in a vast anonymous Nirvana. The Christian hope is that those who leave us only go before, that broken cords of love and fellowship shall be tied again, that life shall resume. An age which, aware that what is called material is dissolving in the physicists' hands, is discovering some sad relevance in Eastern religions, with their vague doctrines of a nameless pool of being into which all life resolves, as dust goes back to dust, can be offered no true hope save where hope was ever found, in the risen Christ. 'We shall be like him,' wrote John in extreme old age, 'for we shall see him as he is.' He had seen him, still Jesus, on the lakeshore – and he had seen the empty tomb in the garden. . . . It was sixty years later, and he still knew.

Hence the continuing popularity of John Henry Newman's best-known hymn, especially the verse with such outreach of faith:

> *So long thy power has blest me, sure it still*
> *Will lead me on*
> *O'er moor and fen, o'er crag and torrent, till*
> *The night is gone;*
> *And with the morn those angel faces smile*
> *Which I have loved long since and lost awhile.*

Newman lived until the age of eighty-nine, and it might have been thought that here was the utterance of evening years. In fact, he wrote 'Lead kindly Light', with all its wistful longing for another world of being, when he was young, for he is said to have expressed dissatisfaction with the hymn fifty years later, perhaps because some metrical structure failed to satisfy his fastidious classicism.

What is of interest is that he must have been young when he wrote it. It seems to have been written when he was on an orange-ship becalmed for a week, of all places, in the windy Strait of Bonifacio, on the way back from Sicily. He spent his enforced leisure writing religious verse. . . . But does not that one stanza express two facets of the yearning of old age, the longing for God's continuing presence, and glad reunion?

From the same deep source of human longing came the imagery of home which haunts many hymns. The traveller grows weary and longs for the rest of home, and assumes that such a place will be a refuge, a warm, familiar place, where dwell those we know. If Newman was young, Tennyson was old. He was in his eighty-first year in October 1889, the year in which Newman died, when, at Farringford, his lovely home in the Isle of Wight, he wrote 'Crossing the Bar'. It is moving to walk up the cliff-top moor, Tennyson's Down, behind the tree-embowered house, to look west down the Channel from the white cliff, and feel convinced that here was the place from which he saw the sunset and the evening star, and heard the call for dinner which brought him from his musings back through the hedge. It was in the evening that he showed the piece to his son, who remarked that it crowned his life's work. 'It came in a moment,' he replied. He died in 1892 and asked, a few days before, that the lovely poem should always conclude any edition of his verse. Picture it, with the day dying on the upward-sloping down behind gracious Farringford:

> Sunset and evening star,
> And one clear call for me!
> And may there be no moaning of the bar,
> When I put out to sea,
>
> But such a tide as moving seems asleep,
> Too full for sound and foam,
> When that which drew from out the boundless deep
> Turns again home.
>
> Twilight and evening bell,
> And after that the dark!
> And may there be no sadness of farewell,
> When I embark;
>
> For, though from out our bourne of Time and Place,
> The flood may bear me far,
> I hope to see my Pilot face to face
> When I have crossed the bar.

It is one of the loveliest utterances of man's twilight years ever written, and contains that yearning for a better life than this which can assail the soul at any season, in loss, in sickness (as in Newman's case), in disappointment, as well as in old age. It is world weariness that makes man sick for real life, stress gone, sorrow quenched, rest won.

It was remarked earlier that the Victorians lived more familiarly with death, and spoke of it more frequently and more emotionally than is done today. Think of the record of the Tait family. Archibald Campbell Tait (1811–82) was appointed to the see of Canterbury in 1868. He and his wife Catherine, who wrote the tragic story, lost five small daughters by scarlet fever in 1856. Catherine herself died in 1878 just after the death of her son Craufurd in his thirtieth year. Both Tait and his wife immediately wrote the story of their bitter loss. So did their contemporary, Archdeacon Brown, who built the lovely mission house, The Elms, at Tauranga, at this world's end, when his son died at King's College in Auckland.

But this leads me to the tragedy of Tait's successor, Bishop Benson, the friend of Gladstone, who succeeded to Tait's see of Canterbury in 1882, because he illustrates my other point, that 'yearning for the other shore' to use Roman Vergil's phrase, which can so strongly sweep upon the soul. I have just read Benson's story of his son, Martin White Benson, again. It always moves me deeply.

Edward White Benson lived for only sixty-seven years, from 1829 to 1896, and tragedy befell him in 1878, the year after he became Bishop of Truro. His son, Martin, whose brief seventeen years were written up in detail by his sorrowing father, died of meningitis (brain fever, they called it in those days) while at school at Wellington College, of which the bishop had been the first headmaster. In his first desperation of grief Benson felt he could never hope to trace the wisdom of God in such sorrow. It was his nature to work out life's problems on paper, so he set out to record the sternest trial to which he had ever been subjected, and found thus some relief. So have I done, as some who read may know.

On his sixtieth birthday Benson confided to his diary that Martin's death was the 'inexplicable grief' of his life, and he wrote a moving little poem which was not found until he died himself seven years later. 'It will be worth dying,' he said, 'to see into it' – and now he had gone to see. The poem runs:

> The martins are back to cornice and eaves,
> Fresh from the glassy sea;
> The Martin of martins my soul bereaves,
> Flying no more to me!
>
> One of them clung to the window-side,
> And twittered a note to me:
> 'There's a Martin beyond o'er wind and tide
> Whom you know better than we.
>
> His nest is hid in a clustered rose,
> On the Prince's own roof-tree;
> When the Prince incomes, when the Prince outgoes,
> The Prince looks up to see.
>
> Calls him hither or sends him there
> To the friends of the Holy Three,
> With a word of love, or a touch of care; –
> Why was he sent to thee?'
>
> Martin I know; and when he went home
> He carried my heart from me.
> Half I remain. Ere Martinmas come,
> Go with this message from me:
>
> Say, 'Thou Prince, he is wholly Thine!
> Sent once on a message to me;
> Yet suffer me soon, at morning shine,
> To see him on Thy roof-tree!'

The archbishop went, found the truth, and surely knew his son. Survival does not make sense on any other terms, and this 'sehnsucht' as the Germans call it, this 'pining', 'yearning' with just a little more than either word contains, is a common experience of age.

Do I look forward to death? I sense the reality of Benson's longing. I catch the feeling of the old Torrey-Alexander song: 'Oh that will be, glory for me . . .' but dying stands between me and death. I was asked the question on television last month in Australia. 'Your friend Malcolm Muggeridge,' they said, 'was here, and we asked him about it. He said he looked forward to death, and gave an illustration – in past days, he said, before flying was the common mode of travel, a few days' voyage by liner across the Atlantic was how one travelled from America back home. At the beginning of the ocean voyage one was interested in a variety of things, whether the cabin had a porthole, whether one was seated at the captain's table, who else was aboard. . . . But when the sea lanes narrowed up the Channel, more and more thought turned eagerly to home. Do you not agree?' asked my interviewer.

'Partly,' I replied. 'I see Mr Muggeridge's point – but what bothers me is immigration, the delay in the grey mist at Tilbury or Southampton, the horrible boat-train, customs, health clearance, and all that lies between the voyage and the joy of home, even the final restlessness, the pacing of the deck.'

My point must be clear. Mr Muggeridge and I were born six weeks apart, I the elder. Our minds probably work in much the same way, and I should be surprised if he never finds some touch of concern in the thought of the manner of his going. Death can come in so many ugly ways. I rather think that this, rather than death itself, was what dogged Samuel Johnson. Mrs Knowles, to be sure, once told him that he should not have a horror for that which is the gate of life. Johnson answered: 'No rational man can die without uneasy apprehension.' His prayers seem to suggest that his deeper concern was over the manner of his passing – 'O God, most merciful father, who by many diseases hast admonished me of my approach to the end of life, and by this gracious addition to my days hast given me an opportunity of appearing once more in thy presence to commemorate the sacrifice by which thy son Jesus Christ has taken away the sins of the world, assist me in this commemoration by thy Holy Spirit that I may look back on the sinfulness of my life past with pious sorrow and efficacious repentance . . . and that I may serve thee with faith hope and charity for the time that thou shalt yet allow me, and finally be received to everlasting happiness for the sake of Jesus Christ our Lord.'

Johnson's prayers show a deep consciousness of sin and imperfection, but that is not reprehensible or morbid. They contain the noblest expressions of faith and aspiration, and those written after his wife's death are most moving in their anguished submission. The great man's last year (he died at the age of seventy-five) was tormented by the physical ills common to that age, and quite beyond its medicine. He was wracked with pain, stupefied with opium. It would be remarkable if anyone so plagued could dissociate a fear of death's processes from death itself. He once said: 'Philosophy may infuse stubbornness but religion only can give patience' – and patience breathes through all the prayers of his last years. We are not called upon to face death with thoughtlessness, nor posing, and that is why, a few weeks before he died, he bade someone write to him no more about 'dying with grace'. And yet, as his very last prayer shows, he faced the end with grace indeed.

But to return more closely to the point. As the field of dying narrows 'between the sunset and the stars', any Christian may well make the last encounter a theme of supplication. Some are privileged to make the transit without pain. 'Haven't you guessed?' asks Aslan in *The Last Battle*, 'there really was a train accident.' They were dead, all the children, but it was a new chapter of a never-ending tale, each one better than the chapter before. When Bunyan's Mr Fearing reached the River it was flowing lower than anyone remembered it before, so that they went across almost dryshod.

'Each chapter better than the last'. . . . What will it be like, that other life? We cannot tell and can only speak in symbol and in imagery. The Bible does no more. 'No one has seen, no one has heard, no one has understood in the depths of his being,' said Paul, 'what God has waiting for those that love him.' Golden streets, eternal light, trees of life by limpid rivers, are all attempts to grasp the edge of what another kind of life can be.

We can see it only in a consummation which is also a beginning. We can be sure that no lovesome, holy experience enjoyed in this life will be lost in another. We can be certain that, if fellowship with a living Christ commences here, it will continue there, and embrace within it all fellowship we have treasured in Christ. Beyond that we are tied, like the writers of the Bible themselves, to symbols – a Celestial City, Aslan's Land, the Mountains of Light. . . .

How seriously, it might be asked, should alleged 'after death experiences' be taken? Perhaps the documentation goes back to Stephen and his vision of Christ, though it might be better to set that apart from experiences more mundane. Dwight L. Moody was brought down with his last illness at the age of sixty-two. It appears, in his son's narrative, to have been obviously a coronary attack. Moody, like his contemporary Charles H. Spurgeon, who died in 1892 at the age of fifty-eight, had lived arduously. It is estimated that he travelled a million miles, and addressed a full hundred million people. To look at surviving photographs of both Moody and Spurgeon is to wish that their burly figures had been under modern medical care.

Moody died on a midwinter day in 1899. In his last hours, his overworked and damaged heart clearly faltering, he drifted in and out of consciousness. On one occasion he said: 'I have seen the children,' referring to the two grandchildren he had lost within a year. Did he, or was it a natural dream of one aware of approaching death?

People pronounced clinically dead who, by medical skill, have been brought back to life, have sometimes spoken of looking down on their bodies and on those seeking to restore life, and of some disappointment at the termination of what seemed to be a joyous transit into some other dimension of existence. How seriously should we regard such stories as 'evidence'? I myself, academically habituated to examine such claims with critical care, should hesitate to found confidence on these tales. The phenomenon could be the result of a temporary deprivation of oxygen in the brain, or to other physiological conditions. The evidence, to my mind, does not stand in the same class as that which convinces me, as a historian, of the resurrection of Jesus Christ. In that is my confidence, there is my solid standing ground. In my conviction that he lives I move forward down the path, long or short as it may be, to the place of meeting. And I speak, I am sure, for many on the last slope of life when I say that my whole concern is the final miles of the journey and the nature of the road.

Do not say to us: 'You still have work to do.' We know that. With weakening hands, but strong, we trust, in will, we try to do it. Above all do not say: 'You will go when your time comes.' That is a Moslem, not a Christian concept. . . . Two friends, they say, were once walking through the crowded Suq in Baghdad when they met Death coming the other way. He looked fixedly at one of them. 'I did not like that,' said the man. 'If I get a fast camel, I can be in Samarra by evening,' and he fled, jostling his way through the crowds. The other man strolled back, and came on Death again. 'Why,' he asked, 'did you look at my friend like that?' 'I was surprised,' Death replied, 'to see him here in Baghdad because I have an appointment with him this evening in Samarra.'

A Christian does not live under such laws. Men do die 'before their time'. Others 'outlive their usefulness', even survive their own minds. I have no answer, nor has anyone, to the dilemma of God's omniscience and human freedom. It is a problem which arises out of the tireless striving of finite minds to penetrate the infinite. God can mould and shape our end as he can control any part of life's pattern, and no rules bind his answers to our prayers, as there is no way of foretelling what he ordains or what he allows. His plans are heaven-high above ours.

Let us simply pray that we shall make a good ending, that there shall be 'some late lark singing', that we may not survive to undo what good we may have done, that our passing may be swift and painless, that we shall not live to be a burden or to lose all purpose in living. May the Great Producer of our life's film step forward suddenly with 'Cut'. Join us in this prayer. It is, and must be our concern. Dismiss us with your blessing.

Chapter Seven

'WE HAVE BUT FAITH . . .'

These musings are what their name suggests, thoughts surely shared by many who march to the same rhythm in the vanguard of humanity. Of that fact I became peculiarly aware in the late sixties, thirteen, fourteen years ago now. Those were strange years, in which a group of sceptical and disillusioned churchmen thought to slay their God and quench the eternal hope of man. I was asked to write in answer to one local contribution to the sombre theme. As best I could, I did. I might do better now that late afternoon has become more sharply evening. But what touched me, even moved me to grateful awe, was the thanks I was honoured with, from the bereaved and the aged, for what they said was the blessed restoration of their faith, that those they loved still lived, as Christ lives, as God lives.

On that hope I have said much, but must say more, for in many lives it assumes at times the sharpest urgency. I quoted Brooke on his mistaken notion of that 'unhoped serene that men call age'. How could he say that, when he thought of death as swinging him 'into the shade and loneliness and mire of the last land', poor man? Serenity, yes, but only if the heart is sure, only if faith stands firm against the surge and thrust of all that comes to challenge it. And where was there ever faith in thinking man without the nagging challenge which comes on darker and more solitary days to test and try it?

When I wrote of Tennyson's *In Memoriam*, I read the whole poem late before the fire, and realised afresh my lifelong kinship with that man. He was the only Englishman, I think, to be given a peerage for his poetry. That is why the two hymns which have been extracted from his poetry touch me at a more sensitive depth than the more jubilant words and confident affirmations of the century before. Tennyson tells us of a faith won from conflict, and, more personally, of confidence torn from the hands of grief and doubt. I have quoted 'Crossing the Bar'. The other hymn is the Prologue to *In Memoriam*, quite possibly written last, when the strife of those sixteen years of sorrow was over, and the writer's spirit reconciled – as I imagine was the First Psalm of the Psalter.

From my earliest Christian experience those verses have gone with me:

> *Strong Son of God, immortal Love,*
> *Whom we that have not seen thy face*
> *By faith and faith alone embrace,*
> *Believing where we cannot prove.*
> ....
>
> *Thou wilt not leave us in the dust:*
> *Thou madest man, he knows not why*
> *He thinks he was not made to die*
> *And thou hast made him, thou art just.*
> ....
>
> *We have but faith; we cannot know;*
> *For knowledge is of things we see;*
> *And yet we trust it comes from thee,*
> *A beam in darkness: let it grow.*

It is dated 1849, the year before Tennyson published the 131 stanzas of the 700 he wrote, and by that writing became poet laureate. But how those three verses helped me as a young Christian in the stress of university study – the affirmation of a Divine Christ, the profound consciousness that man was not made to be dashed down like a broken urn, the clear realisation that faith was a step beyond scientific 'proof'.

I set out, and life-through I have held to the project, to verify belief, to demonstrate proof where demonstration was possible, but faith is a commitment of the life beyond all measuring-device. My faith in God's being, my faith in another life than this, are my deliberate choice between two alternatives. 'Thou art just,' says the line I quote. The propositions hold together. If God is, so is Heaven. Life is no cynical joke, nor an act of tragic injustice.

But how can we picture that other dimension of life save in terms of this, as we said before but relevantly say again? The imagery must be of earth. John's 'elders' in the Apocalypse, sitting by a fire-laced glassy sea, are a memory of the blazing Aegean in the slanting sun as Patmos shows it westward every day. Fields of asphodel, Lewis's paradise of wondrous solidity in the *Great Divorce*. . . . Or Isaac Watts, not far from where Tennyson wrote, looking at the meadows of Marchwood across Southampton Water and picturing 'sweet fields beyond the swelling flood . . . dressed in living green'. The list could go on as devotion, hope and faith have striven to find a language to describe the incomprehensible. But has not the extravagance of such poetic imagery encouraged scepticism? Christians are not Moslems with their houri-haunted heaven. 'There is a land of pure delight,' runs one lush hymn, and 'by faith we can see it afar' – which is plain truth. Many untaught in the ways of language, and how poetry must so often be used as a tool and instrument of thought, can throw out truth with the image used for its communication and expression.

Science, curiously enough, science so wrongly envisaged as the stern vehicle of proven reality, must itself use its models, images and analogies to convey its message. Physicists tell me, if I understand them aright, that what we once called 'matter' as opposed to 'spirit', has vanished through their fingers. As they penetrate the atom, itself admittedly 'rigorously incomprehensible', they reach a strange world beyond all understanding, where all they can postulate is movement. But what is movement, especially movement beyond prediction or pattern, if we do not know what moves? Some add another concept and reach for something which is 'movement plus idea' – a notion, I may add, almost touched upon by the Greek Democritus and his Roman interpreter, Lucretius!

But consider the dilemma. How can there be an idea save that it be in a mind? So how can Ultimate Reality be a vast pool of life or thought or an infinite 'idea' save it be conscious of itself? And back we come to ancient revelation – 'I am that I am,' or 'I am and know I am.' Or consider Descartes' primal thought: 'I think therefore I am.' When the doubter is most secure, and bravely blazing a new trail, he stumbles across God.

It is consciousness that makes life. Consciousness must be the 'living soul' breathed into Adam's clay, as that ancient verse says in language miraculously simple. And it is consciousness which is therefore an essential ingredient to any concept of 'another life'. When our respected Governor-General, Sir Bernard Ferguson, was about to leave us, amid that theological stress of the sixties, he said a parting word to Christians. 'My own belief,' he said, 'which has never wavered in peace or war, is that creatures so complex as we are could never have been called into being for such a brief span on earth as is granted to even the longest-lived of us. . . . I find this much easier to believe than any idea that we are snuffed out like candles or absorbed in some anonymous nirvana.'

It is to such straits that some baffled physicists are reduced in the present quest for meaning in their studies. Such a nameless, unconscious ocean of existence has always haunted the religions of the East. It was a tenet of Stoicism. The soul's spark of being was lost in Being's primal fire. It will not do. If God is personal, so must our survival be. We must know as we are known, or earth is darkness to the core. Is not the agony and the ecstasy, the tingling experience of life, beauty, and all manner of understanding, and, yes, if you will, the pain of grief, sorrow and the manifold distress which purifies the soul, are not these a demanding proof of our continuance? Is it possible that a complicated reticulation, fortuitously assembled, of what we once called atoms, of carbon, hydrogen, oxygen and the rest of the seventeen, could think, agonise, enjoy, write Macbeth, carve Moses, produce *In Memoriam* . . . ?

'By faith we can see it afar. . . .' What is faith? Faith, as a famous chapter in the Epistle to the Hebrews says, 'is the title deeds for things we hope for.' That rendering uses a meaning found by chance in a Greek papyrus in Egypt, but how very attractive it is. The title-deeds can give us present possession of real estate in another land – 'by faith we can see it afar'. Faith is stepping out in the conviction that Christ was what he said he was, God's last demonstration of himself, intruding from another sphere into our space and time, and risen victorious over death. Faith rejects the notion that chance produced the universe, life itself, and all the astounding glory and wonder of it, just so much tumult which, having made itself, will in the end destroy itself; faith cannot accept that Christ was a tragic Galilean who went unnecessarily to execution because he had challenged evil in an entrenched group, and found only betrayal and horrible death. Faith sees a more reasonable alternative – that a mind, a vast intelligence, an enormously majestic force called love, produced all things that are, and seeks to make us free-willed partners in the plan it all involves. And faith commits the life, steps out, acts on this assumption. Faith is a choice. Faith reveals its existence by that choice, a zeal for God, a thirst for goodness. Faith is unswerving trust in God's love, care, involvement. Faith enriches the life, steadies the feet, fathers hope, makes old age as meaningful as youth.

Old age – for to that theme we must return. Perhaps it will surprise the younger, if I deliberately say that there are those who find in age that faith can be tested, challenged, tried more keenly than in earlier years. Not all, I concede. Paul, in his last words, in the second letter to Timothy, which he wrote in AD 67 perhaps, just before his death, spoke in language of utter confidence. He knew that he was near the end. He lay in noisome confinement. There was no chance of acquittal now, as there was in his first detention, house arrest in Rome five years before. And yet he could speak in such confidence in his survival, reward, and hope, that his words have become a classic statement of faith. 'I know whom I have believed, and am persuaded. . . .' He writes in paradox, almost contradicting our line: 'We have but faith, we cannot know. . . .'

But was not John the Baptist as noble a spirit? In his dungeon at Machaerus, he fell into doubt – he, the Messiah's forerunner, a man conscious that he was a figure of prophecy, both in Isaiah and, on the Lord's avowal, in Malachi. He sent to Christ to ask him whether, after all such vast assurance, he could be wrong on the greatest issue of his life. If such a man could be thus tried, need we, in times of loneliness, pain, loss, seeming unanswered prayer, temptation, feel unduly distressed, if the same Dark Enemy comes roaring round our ramparts?

Go back to the same Paul. Pick a date ten years earlier, and read what he says to that turbulent little Church in Corinth. He was worried about their troubles, their dissidence, their unbelief. He was at work in Troas, on the Aegean coast. The opportunities were wide. He was using them effectively. People were pouring into the Church. But so wracked with anxiety was he that, abandoning his work, he journeyed north half way to meet his messenger, and receive assurance thus, a little earlier, that all was well upon the Isthmus. If Paul was anxious, need we consider ourselves strange, sinful, untrusting, folk of little faith, if the clamp of anxiety closes on our heart? Let extroverts without sympathy for the anxious and imaginative refrain from talking of stress and anxiety as sins. And let them think twice, or perhaps three times, before they become judgmental on the theme of fear.

Were the ground not too holy to treat wantonly, I might take you to Gethsemane and the sweat of blood, I might quote the cry of desolation on the cross, and bid the desperate consider that Christ 'was in all points tempted like as we are'. Remember how that awesome statement closes: '. . . yet without sin'. In such times of tension, doubt and even terror, the bounden need is to carry on, to continue the fight, to present an undamaged front to the hostile world and, if we can, shout like Prometheus against the evil power: 'Fiend, I defy thee, with a calm, fixed mind, all that thou canst inflict I bid thee do.' Brave words, much more easy to write down, than, in the right place, to say. Rather than Shelley's dark play read the Psalms. All moods lie there, from 'The Lord is my shepherd; I shall not want' to

'Out of the depths have I cried to thee'. If the Psalms are part of God's Word to us, they sanction the habit which should be for ever ours, of crying out our pain. That habit contains faith in its essence.

Thus, then, must age, especially lonely and harrassed age, deal with attacks upon faith and serenity, such as those I mentioned at the beginning of this chapter coming from those who should have pastored them, a clan about whom Jeremiah would have had some strong words to say. To sum up, here are two lines of thought. One concerns the strong comfort to be found in thinking again through the whole process of faith. Abraham was 'the father of the faithful' and a prime illustration of what the learned writer to the Hebrews has to say. Brought up in that global port, Ur of the Chaldees, converging point for the ships which voyaged east and linked with the very sea lanes of China, and the caravan routes which followed the Fertile Crescent west, and knowing the ships of the Aegean and beyond, Abraham knew well the world, its men, and its lamentable religions. He probably had in his possession tablets of antiquity which told of One God, Creator and Lord, of man in his beginnings and his tragedy. It was thus as Paul saw, and as the Hebrews chapter describes, that Abraham set out to obey a Voice, which bade him found a nation to give such a pure faith to the world. He went, found his 'Promised Land', and then with passing years, under immense stress of disappointment, he doubted, retreated from his destined post, and went to Egypt. Chastened by events, he came back 'to the place where his altar was at the beginning'. So can we. We can, and should, when under trial, go back, think of God, and how he claimed our mind and heart, face the grim alternatives and find, as we will find, that we must reject them again. We should think again of Christ, and ask whether any other verdict on him than the one we were constrained to make when he became personally our Saviour, can possibly be accepted. Thoughtfully, prayerfully, we shall find thus the calm we seek. We are back at the first altar. Let us place our lives on it again – and again if need be.

Such regression also finds argument in our own life's

experience. I have seen too often apparent disaster transformed into victory, what seemed sterile turned to fruitfulness, and a Wisdom at work constructing a pattern of good out of what my observation would have dismissed as confusion, that I am forced to conclude that what now, or what again, seems so meaningless, must find a satisfying conclusion. 'So long thy power has led me, sure it will still lead me on.' I often quote to myself half a verse from a hymn John Newton wrote two centuries ago, with the tempest in mind which had gone far to bring him to Christ:

> *His love in times past*
> *Forbids me to think*
> *He'll leave me at last*
> *In trouble to sink.*

Hence, it may be remarked in passing, the need for good hymns, sound in both their ideas, their truth, and their language. The four lines of Newton which follow those quoted, are too stilted to impress. And observe what damage compilers have done to lines two and four of Keene's two-century-old hymn which can equally steady the soul:

> *The soul that on Jesus has leaned for repose*
> *I will not, I will not desert to its foes,*
> *That soul, though all hell should endeavour to shake*
> *I'll never – no, never – no never forsake.*

So it comes about that, half way through his letter to the Romans, that great document of salvation by faith, Paul suddenly says: 'We are saved by hope.' Faith and hope, in a sense, coincide. We cannot be always looking back. The eyes must be alert on the present battlefield. More, they must look ahead, and can do so in the confidence of faith, on to the consummation. If there is no faith there is no hope, and what is life, especially the end of life, if there is no hope? Despair is the opposite of hope. As Bertrand Russell was clear-minded enough to recognise, without hope, 'it is only on the foundation of unyielding despair' that 'the soul's habitation' can be built.

Neither man nor his society can, on such a basis, permanently subsist. So often, it will be found, those who profess no faith, and hence no hope, exist by some vague expectation that the whole story has not yet been told. It is by a swing of the heel from past to future, or from now to then that faith, in Wordsworth's phrase, 'looks through death'.

Therein too, lies courage, a mighty need. Courage is the antidote to fear. It is the child of faith. It is the practised calmness which faces menace, real or imagined, the will which refuses to retreat. Fear can crowd the evening of life, the more for the imaginative than the stolid. Fear can be both good and bad. There are drugs which take all fear away, so that the drugged attacks an armoured vehicle barehanded, steps from heights, and throws life away. Such poisoning must quench foresight and paralyse imagination. Imagination is not bad. It is part of our humanity. It can as Johnson said, 'satisfy the soul with all luxury, put sceptres in the hand or mitres on the head'. Or it can make the path dark with imagined ills. It has produced all of the glory of man's achievement. It has also paralysed the soul.

It has infinite variety between man and man. I remember once at Timaru visiting a giant freezing works. In an engine room by which we entered was one man. 'May we go in, George?' asked my guide. 'Yes,' said the fellow, pulling off his boiler suit. 'Leave the bar upright. I'll be meeting Tom on the cinder path. I'll tell him you're inside.' It was only when we were inside the huge cool-chamber, hung with ice and frost, and cold with air which hurt the lungs, that the horror of our situation burst on my imagination. Suppose George missed Tom? Tom comes, sees the lockbar on the great door upright, and swings it into its socket. It is Friday night, no cry could be heard outside, we had told no one where we were going. George would find us with the thousands of sheep carcases on Monday morning. All imagination, I know, but at that moment I knew stark fear. I was sweating with horror for all the arctic chill, when we turned back to the door. It swung open. Tom was putting on his boiler suit. I was weak-kneed, but the man who took me into that grisly place had not known a disturbing thought. Such men can die in grotesque accidents.

Fear, therefore, is part of a God-endowed faculty. Adam and Eve might have done better to picture sharply the agony of possible loss of Paradise. David might have done better to fear tomorrow, than envisage enticingly tonight. But all the faculties of our damaged psyche can grow sick and harm us. Like the Lady of Shalott we can fear reality, watch only the reflections in a mirror, and be unable at last without disaster to 'look down to Camelot'. Or we can fear unreality, the pestilence that walks in darkness, and many will testify to the existence of that which can come in the dark small hours to grip the chest almost physically, Fear in its essence.

Courage is the only answer, refusal to be paralysed, a sense of the presence of God, which as Brother Lawrence testified, comes only with its hourly practice, an effort to 'abide in Christ' which is faith's last reach and grasp. True, to know and to prescribe the remedies is much more simple a task than to appropriate and to apply them, a truth which all who write on themes thus personal should make every effort to remember. It is as wrong as it is irresponsible to present an image to those who read one's written words, of unruffled serenity. That can engender despair. At the same time, truth must be written, and a reader may chance to apply it to life better than the one who puts it into words like these.

Who shall say that it is not a terrifying world? Fear and its most vigorous child, hatred, dictate international policies and internal strife. The great can no longer expose their persons in the haunted streets. Perhaps Bertrand Russell was writing words which he could justify, not so many years ago, when he said: 'Our instinctive emotions are those which we have inherited from a much more dangerous world, and contain, therefore, a larger portion of fear than they should.' I do not need to point out that such a diagnosis no longer applies. It was, none the less, in a world not unlike ours, behind long frontiers of fear, that much of the Bible was written. It is in such a context that Isaiah,

Jeremiah, Christ himself said what they had to say. 'Let not your heart be troubled, neither let it be afraid'. . . . 'In quietness and in confidence shall be your strength.'

Let us then seek to keep our eyes on him. Perhaps Peter's adventure may be turned into a parable. When he saw that the sea about him was rough and boisterous, he was 'beginning to sink', when Christ caught hold of him. Let us so reach out 'looking unto Jesus'. Don Oliver, our Olympic weight-lifter, often refreshes me by the simple power of his Christianity, as large and as sturdy as his person. I go to his gymnasium to lift weights and pedal furiously on an exocycle. He told me once how, in an international contest, he failed twice to lift the enormous bar of weights. He had one more chance. 'You are looking at the crowd, Don,' said his manager. 'Look up.' He went out a third time, looked up, high above the crowd, and lifted the weights above his head. Simple, is it not, if we can bring ourselves so to act? I try, I try.

Chapter Eight

'PRAY WITHOUT CEASING'

They can show you on a flank of the Mount of Olives a cave where, the legend goes, Christ taught his disciples the Lord's Prayer. It is one of the least authentic sites of the New Testament. The prayer itself was in answer to a request from his disciples: 'Teach us to pray.' At first sight, such a request for instruction in a process so natural might seem strange. Prayer is, after all, man's instinctive reaction to the pressure of desperate need. Abraham Lincoln once said: 'I have been driven many times to my knees by the overwhelming conviction that I had nowhere else to go. My own wisdom, and that of all about me seemed insufficient for the day.'

Prayer is the breathing of faith. It is communication with one who can hear, and is ready to hear, not a battering at heaven's gate, as the Lord said when he spoke of 'vain repetitions'. 'Baal hear us, Baal hear us.' Nor is it 'getting things from God', as a foolish title I saw once on the back of a book suggested. It is not: 'Listen, Lord, thy servant speaketh.' It is rather the reverse. 'After this manner pray,' said Christ, and he gave in a few words a brief outline of headings which cover adoration, committal and petition. It is a verbal rosary, each phrase of which should be turned over in the mind and conscience, made the theme of meditation and sincere soul-searching. It may be ended at any point, begun at any point. Nothing great or small is uncovered in its sequence. In such a place nothing is great or small.

Prayer is thus a reviewing of the life, the first act in a search for tranquillity. 'Steady then, keep cool and pray,' is

Moffatt's colloquial, but quite legitimate rendering of 1 Peter 4:7. Prayer is a subduing of the soul's storms and rebellions, for can prayer ever end save in the words of the most solemn prayer of all: 'Nevertheless, not my will but thine be done'? There can be stern struggle in the face of that holy capitulation but, after all, is there truer demonstration of the sincerity and reality of our faith save in our willingness to say those words? Read the first seven verses of Psalm 37. What, in the final analysis, for any Christian, is 'the heart's desire'? It is what, in the core of the personality, the deepest sanctum of the soul, we most truly desire.

In the later years of life, prayer can be the chief exercise of the spirit. We have learned by then, perhaps, to pray for what we should properly pray. That, according to Juvenal, the cynical Roman satirist, in his wiser later work, after reviewing the disastrous 'answers' to prayer which he had seen, should be a petition for 'a healthy mind in a healthy body'. Samuel Johnson imitated the passage. Epictetus, who wrote about the same time as Juvenal (he taught Marcus Aurelius, the emperor, Stoicism) said: 'We should look to God and say, Deal with me according to your will. I shrink from nothing that seems good to you. Lead me where you will.' But Christ was not a Stoic, and the Lord's Prayer gives us greater range than this. But under and through all must lie the acceptance of God's will. And that is sometimes a victory to be bought with the soul's blood, and sweat and tears.

Paul knew all about that. It is no wonder that he felt a point of contact with the Stoics, as his Athenian address shows. He writes: 'We know not how to pray as we should but the Spirit pleads for us with groanings which cannot find words.' Thomas could only say: 'My Lord and my God.' Most people who have had a lifetime of experience of God and his ways know that state of mind, a long uplifting of the heart, 'prayer without ceasing', for God's aid, God's over-ruling, God's mercy, a reaching out, a longing mingled with acceptance. Victor Hugo, who lived till the age of eighty-three, once said: 'Certain thoughts are prayers. There are moments when, whatever the attitude of the body, the soul is on its knees.' This is ultimate committal, faith in its living maturity, and it is the remaining task of life to seek this consummation. There should be a purging in such years of the more trivial desires of life, and a conscious preparation for what is soon to be. It is by bathing the mind in the constant presence of God that this cleansing can take place – and sometimes not without trial and tribulation, for there is no discharge in this war.

Some conscious discipline for prayer is, none the less, part of the process. We should seek words, and use them. There are prayers which can and should be uttered, for speech forms and controls thought, and in specifying inter-cession and petition, our desire is clarified and motive purified. There are beautiful liturgies which should be used, even if it is good to keep them short of bondage.

That is the advantage of building prayer (kneeling, walking, sitting – it does not matter) round some phrase of the Lord's Prayer. Contemplation, worship, gratitude, can find a place in the opening words. The mind can stay with one thought or proceed to another. To be sure, prayer can be made at any time, anywhere. Nehemiah shot up a prayer between the Shah's brusque question and the answer. At the same time, it is good to seek silence, not, alas, difficult with the lonely. 'No one can safely speak,' said Thomas à Kempis, 'save the man who loves silence,' and that applies to speech with God, as well as with men. Abraham went to the place where it was his custom to stand before the Lord. Habakkuk, in despair over the murderous rise of imperial Babylon, went to his watchtower to hear what God had to say to him.

I awoke once in my friend's house amid the summer green of Sevenoaks, and turned on the radio. A man was speaking on prayer, and a fine talk he gave. There are times, he pointed out, when a person does not wish to meet anyone, let alone God, but moods are a part of life. Jesus himself had moods, but it is at such times we must pray, for prayer must not be dependent on our variant moods. Prayer, said the morning speaker, is what God says to us, as often as our speaking of what we desire of him. And, indeed, did not Lewis rightly say that God values most those prayers which are prayed in 'dryness of soul'? God can knock on the door of the heart, and we miss blessing if we fail to answer. Let us begin all prayer with God, and scripture aids in this. William Temple said that if he had ten minutes of prayer, he devoted five minutes to thinking about God. Scripture can direct that thought.

I have written elsewhere that 'the Psalter is a book of prayers rather than a prayer book', but anyone can so use it, and familiarity with the Psalms often commands the soul's response. Its words flow on to the pages hot from the heart of man, wracked by pain of body and of mind, or jubilant with joy, despairing, repenting, aspiring, questioning God himself but, and mark this, never ceasing to reach out for God. This is what the radio speaker meant when he stressed the fact that moods should not govern the promptitude of prayer. The psalmists were hungry for God, and that is why, as life moves into its later years, the psalms increasingly become recollected experience, a book which speaks to us in life's peaks and valleys, wave tops and troughs. They can so effectively provide the words contrition, confidence, fear, awe, defeat, and triumph need. 'The Lord is my shepherd . . . '; 'unless I had believed to see the goodness of the Lord . . . '; 'out of the depths I cry to thee . . . '; 'make me to hear joy and gladness; that the bones which thou hast broken may rejoice . . . '; 'praise the Lord, O my soul. . . . '

But in speaking thus of prayer let us avoid the suggestion that, in its depth and comprehensiveness, it is a prerogative of age. No sharp dividing line, as I have insisted, cuts old age off from the rest of life, just as there are no frontiers of time which wall off innocence, happiness, responsibility, success, failure. Storm and trauma can come at any time, and so can stumbling and disaster. Prayer, for those who know themselves, and watch as well as pray, may become wiser, more preoccupied with the doing of God's will than with our daily bread, but it can still diminish or grow as faith does. It is often a 'battleground' – as the Moslems call the prayer alcoves in Istanbul's Blue Mosque.

Bunyan did no service to the mind's peace of such followers as his own Mr Fearing, when he had Ignorance bound and cast away from the very door of the City – 'Then I saw that there was a way to hell, even from the gates of heaven, as well as from the City of Destruction.' But if he meant that there is no point in life at which we can relax our guard, and think that no longer are we 'standing in the need of prayer', he has a point, though I always think that it was not the best way to end his great book. 'There must be a beginning of every great matter,' wrote Drake from Cape Saint Vincent, 'but the continuing of the same to the end until it be thoroughly finished, yieldeth the true glory.'

The lessons on prayer which life can teach have no completion. It was 'an ancient mariner' who learned in Coleridge's famous poem that:

> *He prayeth best who loveth best*
> *All creatures great and small.* . . .

Some difficulties are, indeed, peculiar to age. Francis Lyte did not live past his middle fifties, but he was prematurely old and ill when he wrote 'Abide with me'. He was at grips with the trials of change, and an increasingly alien environment:

> *Swift to its close ebbs out life's little day;*
> *Earth's joys grow dim, its glories pass away;*
> *Change and decay in all around I see –*
> *O thou who changest not, abide with me.*

There is dispute about when Lyte wrote his words on the theme of the Emmaus walk, but surely it was when he left his charge at Brixham in 1844, three years before his death, with 'the sun setting over Dartmoor', as someone wrote, 'and Brixham harbour like a pool of molten gold'. Perhaps the last verse does, in fact, illustrate Edmund Waller's three-centuries-old poem on old age. Put Lyte beside Waller (1606–87), who died a century before Lyte was born in 1793:

> *Hold thou thy cross before my closing eyes,*
> *Shine through the gloom, and point me to the skies:*

92

> *Heaven's morning breaks, and earth's vain shadows flee;*
> *In life, in death, O Lord, abide with me.*

And the poet:

> *The soul's dark cottage, battered and decayed,*
> *Lets in new light through chinks that Time has made;*
> *Stronger by weakness, wiser men become*
> *As they draw near to their eternal home.*
> *Leaving the old, both worlds at once they view*
> *That stand upon the threshold of the new.*

With that, I think, I have little left to say. I set out to write 30,000 words, both because I thought that in such compass I might say everything I really could say without wasting words, and because I think that the Greeks were right: 'Big book, big evil' – they put it in four words. But someone has suggested that I should write some prayers on themes about which I often pray, a risky proceeding. First let me say that it is in words already written that I find much of the framework of petition. I have already in these pages quoted much. Here is more – the first verse of 'Abide with me'. The first line is almost a quotation from that story Luke preserved of the two men who walked into the setting sun, and did not know that Christ was with them:

> *Abide with me: fast falls the eventide;*
> *The darkness deepens: Lord, with me abide;*
> *When other helpers fail, and comforts flee,*
> *Help of the helpless, O abide with me.*

(Dear Lord, as the sun slopes and the feet grow weary, make me sensitive to a Presence on the road, and attune me to listen. It is the voice of stillness which sometimes speaks, not words. Quieten the noise of life around me and let me listen.)

As John Greenleaf Whittier said:

> *Drop thy still dews of quietness,*
> *Till all our strivings cease;*

> *Take from our souls the strain and stress,*
> *And let our ordered lives confess*
> *The beauty of thy peace.*

Whittier, who lived from 1807 to 1892, had not set out to write a hymn. The lovely verse just quoted is in the closing section of a long poem called 'The brewing of Soma', about an Indian drug cult. Less well known is a hymn on the Life Beyond which phrases many a prayer:

> *Thou who hast made my home of life so pleasant,*
> *Leave not its tenant when its walls decay;*
> *O Love divine, O helper ever present,*
> *Be thou my strength and stay.*

If the hymns of writers past their youth are observed, the plea to be lifted above the strife and storm may be often observed. Walsham How wrote 'O my Saviour lifted' as a communion hymn, but it is of far wider appeal. Consider the impact of its last line, faith's last lift:

> *And I come, Lord Jesus;*
> *Dare I turn away?*
> *No! Thy love has conquered,*
> *And I come to-day,*
> *Bringing all my burdens,*
> *Sorrow, sin and care;*
> *At thy feet I lay them,*
> *And I leave them there.*

As Goethe said, in a verse which haunted Oscar Wilde in prison, he who has never 'eaten his bread in sorrow' does not know the strength of heaven. There is a dimension of the soul unknown by those who have never bowed beneath the slings and arrows. They certainly cannot know the agony of prayer, of Psalm 130, for example: 'Out of the depths have I cried unto thee, O Lord. Lord, hear my voice: let thine ears be attentive to the voice of my supplications. . . . I wait for the Lord, my soul doth wait, and in his word do I hope. My soul waiteth for the Lord more than they that watch for the morning.'

'In his word. . . .' My chief memory of the Keswick Convention of 1964 is the singing to slow measure of Number 9 in their hymnal:

> *My Saviour, thou hast offered rest,*
> *O grant it then to me;*
> *The rest of ceasing from myself,*
> *To find my all in thee.*

I spoke in what they call the 'Bible Readings' in that year, and the theme was Mark, the young man who failed but found that 'failure was not final'. The whole of that little Gospel is still laced for me with that moving hymn. 'As if it were not safe to rest and venture all on thee.'

Psalms 23, 27, 37, 51 – I have often thought to do what I have done with some of my favourite poetry – get a little leather-bound book, and write out my own prayer book to carry with me. I should conclude with Samuel Johnson's last prayer – as I should, I think, now conclude this book:

> *Almighty and most merciful Father, I am now,*
> *as to human eyes it seems, about to commemorate,*
> *for the last time, the death of thy Son Jesus Christ*
> *our Saviour and Redeemer. Grant, O Lord, that my*
> *whole hope and confidence may be in his merits,*
> *and thy mercy; enforce and accept my imperfect*
> *repentance; make this commemoration available to*
> *the confirmation of my faith, the establishment of my*
> *hope, and the enlargement of my charity; and make*
> *the death of thy Son Jesus Christ effectual to my*
> *redemption. Have mercy upon me, and pardon the*
> *multitude of my offences. Bless my friends; have*
> *mercy upon all men. Support me, by the Grace of*
> *thy Holy Spirit, in the days of weakness, and at the*
> *hour of death; and receive me, at my death, to*
> *everlasting happiness, for the sake of Jesus Christ.*
> *Amen.*

To which 'Amen', indeed.